BRISTOL, BATH AND WELLS

Then and Now

Peter Laws

BRISTOL, BATH AND WELLS

Then and Now

B.T. BATSFORD LTD

First published 1987

ISBN 0 7134 5259 5

Typeset by Tek-Art Ltd West Wickham Kent
Printed in Great Britain by
R.J. Acford, Chichester, Sussex
for the publishers B.T. Batsford Ltd
4 Fitzhardinge Street, London W1H 0AH

Contents

Acknowledgments 7

Bristol Then and Now 9
Illustrations 18

Bath Then and Now 52
Illustrations 60

Wells Then and Now 88
Illustrations 93

Bibliography 117

Index 118

For Ursula, in the hope that she will enjoy it.

Acknowledgments

I am extremely grateful to so many people for their help and for giving up their time, either in interviews or by correspondence. I thank the following people for photographs: Norman Evans, of The Crown Hotel in Wells, who discovered the Victorian glass-plate negatives in a walled-up cupboard; Arthur and Doreen Hosking of Clevedon for their expertise; Brian Drew of Penzance for his photographs; Dr John Chesterfield of Chacewater; the Bath Reference Library; the staff of the Wells Museum, in particular Anna Baines; Eric Purchase; Michael Griffiths of the Port of Bristol Authority; Leslie Sparks, director of Environmental Services for Bath and his colleague, Mr Davis; L.S. Colchester, Wells Cathedral archivist; Railprint – especially Sue Joslin; Mike Tozer of Pill, Bristol; Madge Soole and the National Railway Musuem; British Rail, Swindon; Harold Harding for the photographs of All Saints, Clifton, and Stanley Nichols of Bristol.

I also thank Michael Overton of the Sally Lunn Refreshment House in Bath; Karin Cross of Weston-super-Mare for her guided tour of Bristol; Jill Knight; Mavis Secrett of the Wells Tourist Office; the planning department of the Mendip District Council in Shepton Mallet; Mike Oakley, assistant county planning officer in Avon; the District County Library in Bridgwater; Barbara Ellis; Derek Sharrocks, Somerset county archivist for the history of the Wells conduit; and Jenny Billington and Sarah Barnes of the Bristol and West Building Society, which is so interested in the historic environment of Bristol. Finally, to Francis Greenacre, curator of fine art in the city of Bristol Museum; Bridget Cherry of The Buildings of England; the County Library in Penzance; Lesley Byrne of The Penzance Library; my wife Stella Laws for all her support and her valuable criticism; Muriel Palmer of Porthleven for her typing and detective work in tracking down plates nos. 33 and 34 (Wells); and the BBC and Stanley Ellis for permission to quote from a radio broadcast.

The photographs are attributed as shown below.

BRISTOL

Arthur Hosking, Clevedon: 2, 6, 13, 25, 26, 31, 52; Dr Chesterfield, Chacewater: 8, 11, 15, 21, 28, 29, 38, 39, 43, 53; F.R. Winstone, Bristol: 9; Brian Drew, Penzance: 16, 18, 19, 32, 41, 50, 56; University of Bristol: 24; John Robinson, London: 37 (Drew), 42 (Drew), 45; Harold Harding, Penzance: 46 (Drew); Newton Freeman, Bristol: 47; Mike Tozer, Pill, Bristol: 48, 49; Port of Bristol Authority: 51; Railprint/ British Rail: 55; Godfrey Soole and National Railway Museum: 57.

BATH

Arthur Hosking: 6, 8, 21; Brian Drew: 13, 34, 44; Bath City Council: 15, 16; Avon County Council: 28, 31, 33, 35 (Frith), 37, 39; Mike Overton, Bath: 30; Ironbridge Gorge Museum: 42; Railprint/British Rail: 43.

WELLS

Wells Museum: 3 (Phillips), 23 (Phillips); Arthur Hosking: 4, 10, 11, 13, 15, 19, 25, 31, 36; Jerry Sampson, Wells: 18; Eric Purchase, Wells: 20, 22, 27, 35; Norman Evans, Wells: 21, 26, 28, 30, 32 (all Phillips); John Oldis, Wells: 33, 34.

All other photographs supplied by the author or the publishers.

BRISTOL

Then and Now

On a cold winter day in January 1983 I made a railway journey from West Cornwall to Bristol to visit a relative in the hospital at Frenchay. Arriving at Temple Meads Station in Bristol, I then took a bus into the city centre and then another bus, making the long trip out through the north-eastern suburbs to the hospital complex. During the five hour train journey I passed the time by reading Keith Brace's *Portrait of Bristol*, the very first page of which contained the following tribute to the city: 'Sir John Betjeman has said that there is no city in England with so much character'. Such a judgement depends on the definition of the word, but that journey from Temple Meads to Frenchay had revealed little else except drab suburbia, so that I wondered at Betjeman's sanity. Two and a half years afterwards, a tour of the city on an open-top bus in August, with a most delightful and informed commentary, helped me begin to make sense of Sir John's words.

Unlike Bath, Bristol had no Roman foundation, but the Romans did establish a small port on the Avon called Abona, about 2 miles (3 km) upstream from its mouth, used as an embarkation point for Wales. Its modern name is Sea Mills and it lies 3 miles (5 km) northwest of the city centre. Six miles (9.5 km) southeast of Abona is the outer Bristol suburb of Brislington where a Roman villa was discovered in 1899 and soon afterwards excavated. Part of the mosaic floor is in the British Museum, and coins found dated it to within AD 250-350.

The Anglo-Saxon word *rige* or *hricg* means a ridge, and from it comes our modern *bridge*, or be-ridge – to erect a structure over a depression. The earliest Saxon names for Bristol are various: Bricstowa, Bricgstow, or Bryogstow in *The Anglo-Saxon Chronicle* for 1051. Some historians dispute the suggested derivation of Bristol as the *Place of the Bridge* – that is, the first bridgehead on the Avon, but it is at least logical and appropriate.

There must have been a settlement here before the Conquest, for the *Chronicle* entry for 1067 records that several sons of King Harold came from Ireland into the Avon, attempted to storm Bristol, but were repulsed, and modern historians claim that the town was a Royal Borough in Saxon England. Yet the most important Saxon district was at Westbury-on-Trym, 3 miles (5 km) north-northwest of the city centre, a Gloucestershire village until absorbed by the city in 1904. Here there was established, *c.* 824, a Benedictine monastery in the diocese of Worcester, and when St Oswald became its Bishop in 961, he reformed the house on the lines of the Benedictine Abbey of St Benoit-sur-Loire, where he himself had been professed. It remained a Benedictine house for over three centuries, and *c.* 1380 the then Bishop of Worcester attempted to establish Westbury as a second diocesan capital, as at Bath and Wells. It failed, and in the fifteenth century Westbury became a collegiate church served by a dean and five prebendaries, one of whom was John Wycliff. Only the fifteenth-century gatehouse now remains and was given to the National Trust in 1907.

The river Avon divided Bristol so that until 1373 its centre north of the river was in

Gloucestershire and the southern centre in Somerset. In return for the services rendered to Edward III at the seige of Calais (the Calais Muster) the Sovereign granted the borough a rare distinction in 1373 by making Bristol an independent county with Shire jurisdiction.

Robert Fitzharding, who became the first Lord Berkeley, founded the Augustinian Abbey in Bristol in 1142, and died as one of its canons. Its main building of the medieval period began in 1298 and was completed by 1330. Further building took place towards the end of the fifteenth century up to 1515.

At this time the borough had a population of about 10,000, and the wealth and enterprise of its merchants developed greatly, the maritime influence extending from Iceland to the Middle East. Wool and cloth were two main exports; wine and iron the main imports. As early as 1350 there were 17 established Guilds, and *c.* 1500, 17 medieval churches within or just without the borough walls.

It was inevitable that the great abbey would end its life as such in the religious troubles of the 1530s, and indeed the end came in 1542. The importance of the borough, nationally, is shown by its inclusion in the list of new sees created that year by the sovereign, alongside Gloucester, Chester, Oxford and Peterborough. Thereafter Bristol became a city, and the abbey church a cathedral, even though it had no nave, and 350 years passed before it was finished in 1888.

In three terrible years during the reign of Mary Tudor (1555-8) 360 men and women were executed for their religious beliefs, five of them in Bristol. Their memorial is to be seen at Cotham Parish Church in the city. Of happier event was the grant in 1552 of a Charter to the Society of Merchant Venturers, founded in the previous century, and the only survivor today of the ancient Guilds. Testifying to the maritime prowess of the Venturers, Bristol was the point from which several famous voyages of discovery started, particularly John Cabot in 1497, and Sebastian Cabot in 1509.

Millerd's map of Bristol in 1671 shows that the urban area covered about 4 square miles (10 sq. km) from St Mary Redcliffe Church in the south, across Bristol Bridge, extending as far north as the Royal Fort, a Cavalier fort built in 1643 by Prince Rupert. (On the site today is one of the finest Georgian houses in Bristol, built in 1761 and still called Royal Fort.) The western boundary of the city was the Cathedral and College Green, whilst the eastern edge was bounded by Lawford's Gate (removed 1769) on the London Road. In all, the map legend mentions 12 gates to the city. Based on High Cross, a magnificent fourteenth-century, 40 ft (12 m) Gothic cross, located at the junction of Broad, Wine, Corn and High Streets, the city lies wholly within a circle half a mile (1 km) in radius, and the map shows 19 churches. Away in the fields in the northeast corner of the map is 'The Pest House', which was an isolation hospital – a very necessary adjunct to a seaport.

The High Cross itself was originally built in 1373; it was decorated with the sculptures of the four Plantagenet kings who had given Bristol its charters. In 1633, the cross was heightened, and four more kings were added – Henry VI, Elizabeth, James I and Charles I – and the whole structure was decorated in gold and other colours. It must have looked magnificent. A century later, the cross was taken down, it is said at the request of a goldsmith who thought that it would fall on to his house, and it was re-erected on College Green, where in 1762 'having proved a source of *annoyance* to the fashionable folk who used the Green as a parade ground, it was again demolished and its parts left lying in the cathedral precincts for six years'. In 1768, the Corporation records say, 'It was disposed of in a most illegitimate manner to a Wiltshire gentleman who used it for decorating the grounds of his house at Stourhead'.

This splendid piece of Bristol history is indeed still in the Park at Stourhead in South Wiltshire, now National Trust property, the cross having been given to the Hoare family by the Dean of

Bristol. Sir Henry Hoare gave the estate to the Trust in 1946. A replica of this High Cross was also set up on College Green in 1850, but this too was taken down and left to deteriorate. The top section, however, was saved, and, now restored, is to be seen in the garden of Berkeley Square, near the University tower.

By 1675 the population of Bristol was second only to London, and these figures indicate its subsequent growth: 1700 – 25,000; 1750 – *c.* 50,000; 1801 – 68,000; 1861 – 179,000, and 1901 – 337,000.

Huge cargoes came into the port in the eighteenth century, mainly of sugar, tobacco and cocoa, hence the Wills and Fry enterprises centred there, all from the West Indies. This eighteenth-century prosperity is reflected in the Georgian development in the city, typified in the building of Queen Square (1700); St James' Square (1707); Orchard Street (1717); Hotwells Crescent (1786), and Portland and Berkeley Squares (1790-1800). There was a great building boom at Clifton at the end of the eighteenth century so that its population rose by 15,000 to 85,000 in the 20 years up to 1820. It was incorporated in the city in 1835, and the Grecian architectural buildings (1820-40) are of outstanding quality.

Of special note is the one building in Bristol by John Wood of Bath, the Corn Exchange (1740-3). Outside this superb Georgian building are the original 'nails' which gave rise to the expression 'to pay on the nail'. They are in effect four bronze pillars with flat tops, used by merchants since the late sixteenth century for business transactions, when bills were paid 'on the nail'. The oldest is 1594 and all of them are inscribed (*see* plate 34). There was a similar custom in the Exchange in Limerick.

In an entirely different style, although about the same period, is Arnos Court (1760-5), a classical villa with Gothick trimmings in Strawberry Hill fashion. Later on, in 1810-11, 4 miles (6.6 km) north of the city centre, is Blaise Hamlet. Here there are ten gabled cottages designed by John Nash for the estate owner, John Harford, and described by Pevsner as 'a subtly informed group of cottages, highly *ornés* and highly Old English'. They were given to the National Trust in 1943.

Despite a letter that John Wesley wrote to the Mayor in 1764, protesting against the proposal to build a theatre in the city, not merely because 'most of the present stage entertainments sap the foundation of religion' but also because a theatre would be 'peculiarly hurtful to a trading city, giving a wrong turn to youth especially', the foundation stone was laid on 30 November 1764 and the theatre opened 18 months later. The architect was Thomas Paty. Just before the opening, certain religious bodies threatened to invoke the provisions of an Act of 1757, so that in order to avoid a threatened prosecution, the opening performance was advertised as 'A Concert of Music and a Specimen of Rhetorick', with a comedy and a farce 'introduced' between orchestral works. King George III granted a Royal Licence in 1778, ten years after he had granted a similar one to the theatre in Bath.

In 1942, the theatre came up for auction, and was purchased by the Council for the Preservation of Ancient Bristol, with a fund raised by public subscription, and placed in trust as a building of national importance. Pevsner says 'internally it is a delight to the eye and a most valuable document of English theatrical history. It is the oldest playhouse in the country still in use as such'. It is a perfect Georgian theatre inside, and the Hanoverian arms are displayed on the proscenium.

Contrasted with this age of fine building and splendid music, there was an ugly black stain on the conscience of Bristol. The Bristolians boasted that they alone kept their trade independent of London, bringing the goods of America into their own port and disposing of them throughout the West Country via their own carriers. So much of their prosperity, however, was linked with the infamous slave trade. Bristol's proud boast of having developed the American colonies was tainted by its dependence on this transporting of humans from West Africa to the Caribbean. Bristol ships laden with goods, often Lancashire cotton, went to the Guinea Coast and exchanged goods for slaves. Slaves, kept in dreadful conditions, were then taken to the West Indies, and the money came back to Bristol plus raw cotton, sugar, cocoa, tobacco and rum. The merchants dined very well and their daughters were taught to play sonatas on the harpsichord by Corelli and Kozeluch.

Horace Walpole wrote in 1750 to Horace Mann:

> We, the British senate, that temple of liberty, and bulwark of Protestant Christianity, have this fortnight been pondering methods to make *more effectual* that horrid traffic of selling negroes. It has appeared to us that six-and-forty thousand of these wretches are sold every year to our plantations alone. It chills one's blood. I would not have to say that I voted in it, for the Continent of America.

Thomas Clarkson of Wisbech published in 1786 an essay against slavery; the cause was taken up by William Wilberforce of Hull, and they were later joined by Zachary Macaulay, father of Lord Macaulay. They succeeded in 1807 when Parliament finally agreed to abolish it, but by then Bristol had virtually abandoned the trade, owing to the American War of Independence and the adverse effect of the French Wars. Keith Brace writes, 'When emancipation of the West Indian slaves came in 1833, Bristol's interest suffered a death blow, and the city went into the long decline of the early Victorian period'.

Two years before, in 1831, the great Bristol Reform Riots took place, in which many people died and property was destroyed. They were partly a vendetta against the Recorder, Sir Charles Wetherell, who opposed the Reform Bill. He came to open the Assizes on 29 October, and that night terror resulted. For three days Bristol witnessed the worst outbreak of urban rioting since the anti-Papist Gordon riots in London in 1780. These riots were thought to be the result of a clash betwen the locals and the wealthy merchants who kept control over an unreformed town council. The young Isambard Kingdom Brunel was in the city at the height of the riots on 30 October; he was enlisted as a special constable and helped to salvage plate from the Mansion House. The riots led to the reform of the council with the Municipal Corporations Act of 1835, which established an elected council for the city. The cost of the riots, however, was inordinate, and, consequently, the planned project of the Clifton Suspension Bridge was delayed for five years.

The idea of throwing a bridge across the near-vertical sides of the Avon Gorge at Clifton was first mooted in the 1750s, and it was the suspension bridge design by Brunel that was accepted by the competition judges in March 1831. The competition was sponsored by the Society of Merchant Venturers, and £8000 had been raised by 1829. Having agreed to the design, the Society's Bridge Committee was anxious to start – the first sod was turned on 21 July 1831. It soon became apparent that less than half of the cost, £52,000, was available. By 1843, £40,000 had been spent, a further £30,000 was necessary, and only the two piers had been built.

Much earlier, Brunel had built a suspension bridge across the Thames at Charing Cross between 1841-5, and he had had the iron chains made by Cornish foundrymen at the Copperhouse Foundry in Hayle, who were reputed for their excellent work. When that bridge was dismantled in 1861 to make way for the new SE&CR bridge, these chains were purchased by a new Bristol Company whose object was to complete the bridge at Clifton as a memorial to Brunel, who had died in September 1859. This magnificent bridge was finally opened on 8 December 1864, and it hangs today on 162 chains or suspension rods, most of which were made in Cornwall in 1840. A typical rod of hand-wrought iron measures 25 ft x 7 in x 1 in (6 m x 18 cm x 2.5 cm), and the clear span of the bridge is 702 ft 3 in (214 m). Not only is it a tribute to Victorian craftsmanship, but it still gives pleasure and is used by thousands annually, although over 120 years old.

The year 1836 in Bristol was marked by a strange occurence – the city lost its Bishop. Henry VIII had established the see in 1542, but with a very inadequate endowment. The Augustinian Abbey church had only a chancel, Lady chapel, north and south transepts, and a crossing tower by 1515, when work was started on the nave. The unfinished state of the building led diocesan bishops to regard the cathedral as a stop-gap from which they moved on to more important offices. This squat building brought about such descriptions as 'mean' (Defoe) and 'the Cathedral which has nothing fine or curious about it!' (Celia Fiennes).

Consequently, in the last year of the reign of William IV 1836, the see of Bristol was united with that of Gloucester; this decision may have been prompted by the destruction of the Bishop's Palace during the riots. Although the diocesan had gone, the cathedral was still maintained. In 1850 the dean invited Brunel to examine defects in the fabric; typically, the restless Brunel informed the dean that he could meet him only at 5 a.m. on a summer morning to survey the fabric because he had to catch the 7.50 train to Exeter. The appointment was duly kept.

In 1866, largely through the work of Archdeacon Norris, the project of completing the cathedral by building the nave was mooted, and the great Victorian architect George (later Sir George) Edmund Street presented to the Restoration Committee a fine design for both nave and western towers with small steeples. After Street's death in 1881, John Loughborough Pearson (architect of Truro Cathedral 1880) completed the towers, but the steeples were omitted.

In the year of the Queen's Diamond Jubilee, the zealous efforts of the citizens of Bristol raised £60,000 and a successful appeal was made to Parliament to re-establish the see; and the first bishop of the revived diocese, Dr George Browne, was enthroned on 28 October 1897. The exterior cleaning of the whole cathedral in 1970 gave the building a new charm.

The presence of carboniferous limestone at Bristol gave the city the advantage of a local coalfield which was a key factor in Bristol's prosperity in the eighteenth century. The place-name Coalpit Heath, only 7 miles (11 km) northeast of the city centre, is self-explanatory, and coal was dug within the city boundary in this century. One of the earliest railways was built in 1803 to carry coal from this Bristol coalfield to the River Avon – the Avon and Gloucester Railway.

Another early railway, of famous status, owes its origins to Bristol – the Great Western. The same group of enterprising Bristol merchants who had promoted the Clifton Suspension Bridge in 1829, including such personalities as Robert Bright, Peter Maze and Thomas Guppy, were the backers of the new railway, ably supported by Charles Russell and C.A. Saunders of London. They appointed the 27-year-old Isambard Brunel as engineer, and the Great Western Railway Act received the Royal Assent on 31 August 1835. In five years the line to Bath was opened, and by June 1841 it had been extended to London. Three years later the rails had reached Exeter, and Plymouth in 1848.

Brunel was not only a railway engineer; he was in all things an engineer *par excellence*. Because of his enthusiasm and that of Peter Maze, a Bristolian with interests in cotton, the GWR directors established the Great Western Steamship Company in 1835 – the 'extension' of the railway from Bristol to New York by way of a ship – and its first ship, the *Great Western*, was built in Bristol and launched in July 1837. The maiden voyage to New York was made in April 1838, and the ship became a success. A sister vessel was soon conceived, the *Great Britain*, and work began on this in July 1839. On 11 December 1844 she left Bristol, not to return for 125 years. Amongst the board of directors responsible were Peter Maze, the Chairman, Henry Bush, Robert Bright, and T.R. Guppy, all concerned with the start of the GWR.

The *Great Britain* was a pioneering vessel — the first ocean-going ship to have an iron hull and a screw propeller. She was also the first ship to have a six-bladed propeller, a semi-balanced rudder, wire rigging, an *electric* log, a double bottom, transverse watertight bulkheads, folding masts and a hollow wrought-iron propeller shaft. In addition, she was the largest ship afloat.

In all she made 44 voyages, and on her last started out from Penarth in South Wales on 6 February 1886, bound for San Francisco via Cape Horn. When she reached the Cape she ran into a hurricane which did so much damage that the crew persuaded the captain to put back to the Falkland Islands. There she remained for 50 years as a hulk for wool and coal storage. On 14 April 1937, the hulk was towed out from Port Stanley, a few miles to Sparrow Cove, there scuttled so that it settled down comfortably on to the sea bed.

On 17 September 1968, *The Times* carried a photograph of the hulk of this pioneer ship with the remains of three masts standing up from the deck, with the caption 'Brunel's great ship may return to Britain'. In 1967 the naval architect Dr Ewan Corlett, who had been interested in the ship since 1952, described her in a letter to *The Times* as 'the forefather of all modern ships'.

On 7 April 1970 she was refloated, placed on a pontoon and towed 7500 miles (12,000 km) back to Britain, passing Scilly on 21 June. Finally, on 19 July, the 127th anniversary of her launch, she was inched gently back into her original dock. It was an amazing success story by an Anglo-German team. This marvellous ship is now well on the way to complete restoration (*see* plate 52).

On 6 March 1865, a new railway was opened from a station beneath the Clifton Suspension Bridge along the Avon Gorge to a terminus at Avonmouth, 5 miles (8 km) away. It was born at the time of the first concrete proposals for erecting a quay at Avonmouth. Development began at last in 1868, and Avonmouth Dock was completed in 1877, when liners started coming up the Bristol Channel to the new dock as part of the great boom in shipping in the last quarter of the nineteenth century. The day that the new dock came into service, 24 February 1877, this hitherto isolated railway was joined up to the GWR. Avonmouth Dock soon became a discharge point for huge quantities of wheat from America, frozen meat from the Argentine, cocoa for Fry's and tobacco for Wills, not to mention the huge cargoes of bananas from the West Indies. In 1970, there were 7 miles (11 km) of quays and wharves, serviced by a labour force of nearly 1400, and 40 years before, there was a passenger rail terminal here alongside the entrance lock 'fully equipped with Customs, baggage, examination, and waiting rooms, and is in continuous use for passengers to and from the West Indies and Central America, and occasionally Australia and New Zealand. The special train journey between Paddington and Avonmouth occupies only two hours.'

In 1929, more bananas entered Avonmouth in the port of Bristol than any other European port, about 900,000,000, and there were special banana trains to deal with this tremendous traffic. I was walking over the summit of Blisworth Hill in Northamptonshire, 15 years ago, *through* which the longest canal tunnel in Britain (3056 yd [*c.* 2750 m]) was bored in the 1790s, when I came across a derelict railway line. It was part of the Stratford & Midland Junction Railway. A local railwayman related that LMS Banana Specials used this curious route at one time to bring bananas across the country – Avonmouth, Evesham, Bidford-on-Avon, Towcester, Stoke Bruerne and Olney to Bedford. This is confirmed in J.M. Dunn's history of the railway.

The prosperity of this city in the latter half of Victoria's reign is reflected in fine public buildings erected for many institutions and organisations. In 1850 there was formed the Bristol Society of Architects, and after an alliance with the Academy of Fine Arts, splendid new premises were built in Queen's Road, completed in 1857. Some members favoured Neo-Greek, others the Italian style, so, inevitably, with the British love of compromise, the exterior was rendered Italian by John Hirst and the interior all Greek by Charles Underwood. It is now the Royal West of England Academy of Art, about which Keith Brace remarked – 'architecturally one of the city's most bizarre buildings'.

In 1861, the Colston Hall Company was founded with the object of providing a concert hall for the city. The name commemorates Edward Colston, born in the Temple area of Bristol in 1636. A vast building was then completed in 1867 to the design of John Foster and John Wood, its great hall a mixture of Byzantine and High Renaissance, so that the costs exceeded the Company's resources. It was destroyed by fire in 1898 and rebuilt.

The judiciary had urged the building of new Assize courts in the 1860s, but the Corporation mis-handled their architectural competition, stating that there was no guarantee of acceptance of any scheme submitted, and there were two separate sites into the bargain. They received only one scheme! A site was then agreed in Small Street, but there was much more trouble to come. A second competition was held when the assessor awarded the first, second and third schemes to one architect, who had submitted designs in three styles! Much anger was expressed by the Presidents of the RIBA and the local Society. Yet a third competition was held, again with another assessor, and the building that exists today was the result. The architects were T.S. Pope and John Bindon, and the building was completed in 1870. It is in the grand High Victorian Gothic manner.

The University College was founded in 1876 as the College of Science and Literature, receiving its charter in 1909. The architect Charles Francis Hansom (who designed Clifton College in 1862) did publish a design for the proposed Medical School in 1880, but this first University building, when erected, did not conform to his design, although containing the same elements. Other buildings followed in Edward VII's time. Part of the University complex includes the building completed in 1871 to serve jointly the Bristol Library and the Philosophical Institution. The architects were John Foster and Archibald Ponton, and to quote Pevsner 'It is the greatest compliment the West Country paid to John Ruskin'. The style is unmistakingly Veronese Gothic. It is now used as the University refectory.

The glory of the University is the main building in Queen's Road, completed in 1925, and given by Sir George Wills and Henry Wills, sons of the first Chancellor in the University. The architect was Sir George Oatley (1863-1950), who was trained in the office of Thomas Dashwood in the Isle of Wight, and who was approached by the donors for a design just before the Great War. Building work was resumed about 1919 and was opened by King George V in the summer of 1925. The great Gothic tower (*see* plate 25) is one of the landmarks of Bristol and was built of Bath and Clipsham stone.

Alongside the main railway line, 3 miles (5 km) from the east portal of the Severn Tunnel, are the Cattybrook brick works, founded in 1865 by Charles Richardson, engineer of the Bristol and South Wales Railway. He was also Chief Engineer for the tunnel, built between 1873 and 1885, and he used 30,000,000 bricks from his own works for the lining; 70,000 sq. yd (58,530 sq. m) or 14½ acres (6 ha) of brickwork has still to be kept pointed by British Rail. One of the Cattybrook products was a deep red brick, used for the Wills' tobacco warehouse in Bedminster by the architect Frank Wills in 1888. He also designed the City Art Gallery (1899-1904) about which Pevsner says 'in a kind of moderate Baroque!'.

William Morris, Philip Webb, Norman Shaw and John Dando Sedding, together with his brother Edmund, had all been trained in the architectural practice established in Beaumont Street, Oxford, by George Edmund Street. They all represented Street's love of craftsmanship and inherited his delight in using iron, stone and timber. Edmund Sedding was in Bristol in 1860, as Precentor of St Raphael's College, founded in 1855 as almshouses for aged seamen. He moved to Penzance in 1861 for the sake of his health, and set up in practice as an architect, where his brother John joined him in 1863. After Edmund's death in June 1868, aged only 36, John returned to Bristol and became an architect of importance until his own death in April 1891 at Winsford Rectory in Somerset, where he had been surveying the church for restoration.

It was a time of revival of the religious communities in the Anglican Church, and the Order of the Sisters of Charity had been founded in Bristol in 1869. They cared for poor and destitute children. By 1890, the Order needed a House of its own, and John Sedding, skilled in church architecture and a good High Churchman, designed their new convent in Redcatch Road, Knowle, in *c.* 1890-1. Unlike any other building in Bristol of the '90s, it revealed Sedding's flair for vernacular architecture with such delights inside as patterned plaster ceilings, wide inglenooks and stone passages.

Before his death, his brother's son, also Edmund, had joined him, together with Henry Wilson who added a refectory in 1903, whilst George Bodley had built the chapel in 1900.

Completing this section on Bristol buildings is Charles Holden's Central Library. Holden was born in 1875, and trained by C.R. Ashbee, and was destined to become well-known as the architect for London Transport tube stations in the 1930s, e.g. Sudbury.

The east elevation of Bristol Library in Deanery Road, which was built in 1906, clearly derives from the work of the Art Nouveau Scots architect, Charles Rennie Mackintosh (1868-1928).

During World War II, and particularly in the autumn of 1940, there were terrible air raids at Bristol by the Nazi bombers. The date 24 November 1940 was described as catastrophic, when the damage done to the city was greater than to most of the big cities of Britain. The greatest architectural loss to Bristol was that of St Peter's Hospital. This building was originally built *c.* 1400 and was the residence of Thomas Norton, an alchemist *c.* 1500. It was a typical medieval building with overhangs, oriels and gables – a style that lived on in Bristol until late into the seventeenth century, viz. Llandoger Trow of 1669 (*see* plate 1). After use as a residence, it became a sugar refinery, and then a royal mint, producing silver coins *c.* 1690. In 1698 it was acquired as a workhouse for 'indoor paupers', then it became a Board Room for the Poor Law Guardians, and finally a Register Office. This was one of the fine buildings completely destroyed in November 1940. The cost of the raids was: 1299 citizens killed, 3000 homes destroyed and 90,000 damaged. It was written of the centre of Bristol *c.* 1947 'the problem of replacing the centre of the old city was enormously simplified. Enemy bombs had cleared the site for us.' In a broadcast in June 1985 on BBC Radio 4, Stanley Ellis, Honorary Fellow in the University of Leeds, said 'The heart of the city was torn out by bombing in the war, and roofless churches – by the dozen, almost – stand as witnesses; empty eyeless monuments, overwhelmed by some of the most ugly or the most eccentric sixties or seventies buildings, that I can remember seeing anywhere'. Pevsner also commented in 1958 'Housing estates spread everywhere on the outskirts and look exactly like those of Birmingham or Nottingham.'

It is with relief to record that the great church of St Mary Redcliffe – called by Queen Elizabeth 'the fairest, goodliest, and most famous parish church in England' – that almost endeavours to be a cathedral, was unscathed. It was built over two centuries commencing *c.* 1294, although the 292 ft (89 m) spire was not completed until 1872. The word 'Redcliff' derives from the red sandstone terrace on which it was built, and indeed Red Pennant Sandstone is still quarried in the Hanham Gorge southeast of the city, a material that has been used for Bristol buildings for centuries.

Stanley Ellis was stringent in his criticism of modern buildings, and despite the enthusiasm of the exponents of 'brutalism', it is difficult to be eloquent about the Colston Centre (1972); but on the credit side, however, the fine new Sun Life building at St James Barton is clad with a delightful golden stone. On Narrow Quay, a huge tea warehouse of the 1830s built of local stone has been splendidly converted to provide new quarters for the Arnolfini Arts Centre, and architects' offices. This is an excellent example of an old building conserved and adapted for a new use. It can be seen behind the ship *Golden Hind* in plate 53.

This great city, granted a Lord Mayoralty by the Queen in 1899, still grows. It covered but 4 sq. miles (10 sq. km) in 1671; three centuries later it had 42 sq. miles (109 sq. km) inside its own boundaries, and its population of 266,000 in 1881 has grown to 399,000. It was sad, therefore, to read in 1983 'that Bristol's docks are gradually changing into a recreation area'.

The riots in the St Paul's area of the city in the 1980s are symptomatic of an age of urban decay, poor housing, social deprivation and general malaise. One can but hope that the Government, and society, will heed the warnings thus displayed, and react (and act) accordingly.

As a footnote, one of the Saxon names for the city was Bricgstow, that has become Bristol with the intrusion of the legendary addition — the Bristolian 'l' to words ending with a vowel, such as 'cameral'. A Bedminster tobacco worker married a girl from Mangotsfield that he called Monocle, and she bore him three girls who were known as Idol, Evil and Normal (Monica, Ida, Eva and Norma)!

1, of *c*. 1900, shows the main façade of the range of buildings known as The Llandoger Trow in King Street, which was laid out *c*. 1663 at the time of the Restoration. They date from 1664, and are historically the most valuable of their kind in Bristol. Records show that the name was known in 1775, and it comes from the flat-bottomed barge called a trow in use on the Severn. A Captain Hawkins traded from the nearby quay called the Welsh Back across to Llandogo on the Wye, several miles upstream of Tintern (where trows were built), and he retired to run this licensed house, one legend claiming that the name came from his ship. The inn has also been linked with the 'Spyglass Inn' in Stevenson's *Treasure Island*.

1

2 (1985) During the Second World War, the two eastern gables of this 'eminently picturesque' (Pevsner) building were destroyed during the Nazi aerial bombardment of the city. In 1962, the remaining three were extensively restored, and preserved for the future by Berni Inns, a good example of a new use for a historical building that has in no way destroyed the character. Inside are to be seen many playbills from the nearby Theatre Royal, spread over six generations, as well as those announcing slave auctions, a ghastly trade in which Bristol played a major part from the late seventeenth century until its abolition.

2

3

3, taken about a century ago, shows the Commercial Rooms in Corn Street, the heart of Bristol's business district. These were opened in 1811 as a coffee house or merchants' club, the first President being John Loudon McAdam (1756-1836), the Ayrshire Scot who pioneered road building and who was appointed Surveyor-General for the Bristol Roads in 1815. The architect of this splendid Greek-revival building, reminiscent of Soane, was C.A. Busby, who later became famous in Brighton. Here was set up in 1852, Bristol's first telegraph office. The three statues are by J.G. Bubb.

4 shows the Rooms today; note that the windows, from which the Victorians had removed their glazing bars, have been properly restored. The four gas lamps have gone and the building shown on the left-hand side of the older picture is no longer extant. Keith Brace says of this Institution:

> inside is the large club-room fitted with armchairs and a fine ceiling with lantern and dome, and a now rather superfluous wind indicator . . . a general feeling that how irrelevant to the great movements of modern finance, this is how business should be conducted.

4

5 is a photograph taken about 1950 of nos. 1 and 2 James Place in Hotwells, at one time a pair of elegant houses of the late eighteenth or early nineteenth century, in the heyday of the Hotwells Spa. The veteran Bristol historian, F.R. Winstone, said of this photograph:

House without an Owner? No. 2 James Place, Joy Hill, Hotwells, Bristol has fallen into such a condition that Bristol Corporation find it a public danger but cannot trace the owner. The City Architect is anxious to restore and preserve what was a fine example of Georgian architecture.

6 shows the place in 1985. It is particularly sad to note that the buildings have both gone, and that the site is derelict – almost unbelievable in these days of very high values of inner city building sites.

5

6

7

7 and **8** indicate the waterside character of Clifton on the bank of the Avon. **7** was taken *c.* 1930. Note the steam roller in Hotwell Road and what appears to be a pier or jetty on the left-hand side of the picture.

The contemporary photograph (**8**) shows just how much has survived of this scene, but the pier has gone, as have many riverside buildings to the left of the elegant terrace on the left-hand side of the picture. In the centre of the older photo is a large plain building with few windows. That has gone, replaced by a block of flats in the contemporary style.

8

9

9, 10 and **11** Hotwells, the Spa of Bristol, was based on a well near the bank of the Avon, its waters first described by the Bristol chronicler William Wyrecestre, in the fifteenth century, and its social life in 1634, four years after the grant of the first baths licence. It became well-known by 1675 for the treatment of kidney ailments and diabetes. Even Catherine of Braganza, consort to Charles II, and Sarah Duchess of Marlborough visited the Spa, but it was a sad place because it was regarded as a last resort when all else had failed. One set of local lodgings was known as Death Row.

But there was an orchestra, riding, boat trips, races on the Downs above, and of course, delicious scandal. It all went into decline in the early part of the nineteenth century.

9 shows Hotwell House of 1816, the bath house that replaced the earlier pump room of 1696, itself demolished in 1867 when the river was widened. On the extreme right-hand side of the picture is the end of the Colonnade, a charming curved crescent of 1786, although never completed, based on Bath Street in Bath. In front of the recessed ground floor is a sheltered promenade with the roof supported on columns.

10 is of *c.* 1930, when there were still trams. Note that the end section of the Crescent has disappeared. Thankfully, this remaining part of the Spa is still extant (**11**), exactly 200 years old, refurbished and more cheerful 'than when it lodged consumptive beauties risking the night damp to attend some over-heated Dance of Death in the Assembly Rooms' (Brace).

10

11

12

12 and **13** No greater contrast could be found than between these two photographs. **12** shows old Bristol with its cobbled street and historic buildings, yet the picture was taken less than 40 years ago.

George Whitefield was born at the Bell Inn at Gloucester on 16 December 1714. He became a Servitor (student doing menial duties) at Pembroke College, Oxford, and matriculated in November 1732. At Oxford he joined up with Charles Wesley (1708-88) and was admitted to the 'Methodist Society' in 1735. In June 1736, Bishop Martin Benson ordained him deacon in Gloucester Cathedral after he had graduated as a BA the previous July. In November of that year, he became a curate at the parish church in the village of Dummer in northeast Hampshire, a place much in the limelight 250 years later when the squire's daughter, Sarah Margaret, became HRH The Duchess of York, and daughter-in-law to the Sovereign.

In 1748 he was appointed chaplain to the Countess of Huntingdon and founded the Calvinist Methodists. He risked his life to bring Christian living to the oppressed Bristol coalminers, and opened this Tabernacle Chapel in Penn Street, 1753. Here was born the Missionary Society (later the London Missionary Society), and opposite was the first Meeting House of 1670 that the Quakers built, in the ruins of the medieval Dominican Friary dissolved in 1542. In this house, in 1696, William Penn, founder of Pennsylvania (hence Penn Street) was married.

In the post-war redevelopment of Bristol, this historic chapel and its Sunday School of 1834 were demolished, against a background of considerable local opposition.

13 shows the place today – just another city centre shopping area, of little character.

13

GOLD
FLAKE
FISH & CHIP RESTAURANT

15

14 Here, in perhaps the most picturesque part of the old city, is an arched gateway of the fourteenth century, a precious fragment of the convent and hospice of St Bartholomew, founded before 1207, for old sailors. On one side of it is a very defaced statue of the Virgin Mary, in the Wells style.

Over the arch is a seventeenth-century house, where after the dissolution of the hospice in 1532, in an earlier building, Bristol Grammar School was founded by Royal Charter (Henry VIII) to remain until 1769. Since the archway was on Horse (now Host) Street, the only direct way out of the medieval city, the scholars greeted Queen Elizabeth I here in 1574 on her way to the cathedral.

15 The arch leads into a narrow stepped street, Christmas Steps (not unlike Clovelly), of small shops, at the summit of which there is a plaque commemorating the laying-out of the street in 1669 by the public-spirited Sheriff Jonathan Blackwell.

16 shows the archway in 1986. A comparison with **14** reveals that the building on the left is still a fish and chip shop, but it has been beautifully restored and the medieval timbering exposed. The building on the right is still a confectioner, newsagent and tobacconist, and it too has had a beneficial facelift. To its right is an ugly piece of 'brutalism' which could well have been avoided.

16

BOVRIL
BOVRIL

18

17, 18 and **19** The Temple area takes its name from meadows or meads given to the Knights Templars in 1145, and they have given the name to the famous railway station nearby, Temple Meads. Here the Knights built their oval church; but when the Order was suppressed in 1312, the Knights of St John took over and rebuilt the church, which was the Guild church of the weavers, fullers and tuckers, who abounded in this area of the city. Its great 114 ft (35 m) tower, begun in 1300, has a lean of 5 ft (1.5 m) caused by subsidence when it was half-finished, completion being suspended for two generations. Here John Wesley preached, and on it rained down fire and high explosive from Hitler's air armada.

17 is a fine Kersting picture of about 40 years ago that shows the tower from the south and part of the ruined nave. The second picture, **18**, is the same view today. Sitting in the tree-girt churchyard, now a greensward, on a hot sunny afternoon in August 1985, I noted:

> All around is the din of modern road traffic that when one is nearer to it dulls the senses. In this green quiet place dominated by the great tower and ruins of the church on which the Teutonic fury of Goering was unleashed in 1940, there is a reminder of Bristol in the early Middle Ages.

In a BBC radio broadcast about Bristol in June 1985, Stanley Ellis said: 'roofless churches overwhelmed by some of the most ugly buildings that I can remember seeing anywhere'. **19** exemplifies this.

19

20

21

22

20 shows the tower and steeple of the Church of St John Baptist at the northwest end of Broad Street. The church is also referred to as St John-on-the-Wall, since it was actually built into and over the city wall, and over St John's Gate, the last survivor of the city's 17 gates. Here Queen Elizabeth entered the city in 1574 riding on a white horse.

The original building was founded in 1174. Today it consists of a crypt, entered from Nelson Street, level with the wall and used for parish purposes, and over it the church consisting of a nave and chancel. The east part of the crypt is probably twelfth-century, the west part and the nave erected by Walter Frampton (died 1388) whose effigy is in the church, with two angels and his long-tailed dog at his feet. The chancel is post-1475. On each side of the upper part of the archway are two effigies of Gaulish chiefs, Brennas and Belinus, said to have founded the city in 390 BC.

21 shows the tower and gateway in 1985, dominated by a modern tower-block that dwarfs the church. **22** shows the church from the northwest, with its attendant tower-blocks that have so little architectural character.

23 shows Bristol's most stylish shopping street, Park Street, which is exhaustingly steep. In the centre of the photograph a large Union Jack hangs from a building, and it is believed that this was for the impending Royal visit in June 1925 by King George V to open the new University Tower and adjoining buildings. Projecting from all the shops on the right-hand side are huge name boards, some protruding as far out as the roadway. In the bottom right-hand corner is a splendid landaulette of perhaps 1913.

24 is a photograph taken on that summer day in June 1925 when King George V came to Bristol. The city was *en fête* and sightseers were to be seen from upstairs windows in Park Street and even from the high parapet gutters below the mansard roofs.

25 shows this scene in 1985. The name boards have gone, and the motor cars are dull in comparison. The one dominant feature common to both is the great Gothic tower of the University, which was founded in 1876. The architect of the tower was Sir George Oatley LLD, FRIBA, of Bristol, and his work is 'a remarkable piece, proof of the architect's unfaltering faith in the Gothic style and up to the boldest displays of Yale' (Pevsner).

26, **27**, **28** and **29**
Northwest of the cathedral is the green expanse of Brandon Hill, a 29 acre (12 ha) public park purchased by the Corporation in 1625, on which traditionally there was a chapel dedicated to St Brendon. He was an Irish abbot at Killeedy in Co. Limerick who died in 577, and who the Irish believe sailed across the Atlantic in an ocean-going leather boat (curragh) to discover America. Tim Severin did just that in 1976 between Brendan Quay Co. Kerry, and Halifax, Nova Scotia, to prove its feasibility.

On the summit of the hill is a spectacular tower designed by the Bristol architect William Venn Gough in 1896, and completed in 1898; it has been described as Gough's triumph. He used red sandstone for the construction, and it has an ascent of 109 steps to the top viewing balcony. Pevsner says of it 'square and slender, the details going more unconventional Gothic as the tower rises. Canopied balconies and short spire surrounded by bristly pinnacles'. It was erected to commemorate the fourth century of the voyage from Bristol of John and Sebastian Cabot of Venice, who traded with the city, and who together saw the coast of Labrador in 1497.

26

27

28

26 shows the tower, and **27** is a panoramic view from its summit looking southeast *c.* 1930. Prominent in the centre is Bristol Cathedral, founded as an Augustinian abbey in 1142, and a cathedral since 1542. The chancel and central tower were built between 1298-1515, but the nave and western towers not until 1868-88, to the design of Sir George Street, and after his death, J.L. Pearson. The tall spire visible in the picture is that of the noble church of St Mary Redcliffe (thirteenth- to fifteenth-century), and to its left, one of the city's 'glass-cones' or bottle-kilns.

28 shows the same panorama today, the long curved building in the foreground being the Council House designed by E. Vincent Harris. Its foundation stone was laid in 1935, work proper began in 1938, and the building was opened by the Queen in 1956. The cathedral is still prominent, but the tower and spire of St Mary Redcliffe are hidden amid a jumble of tower blocks that now spread across the whole prospect.

29 shows the view from the summit looking northeast, the University Tower in Park Street prominent on the left-hand side.

30

31

32

30, 31 and **32** The five city centre churches – All Saints, Christ Church, St John Baptist, St Nicholas and St Stephen – are as fine as many city centre churches in London. Their congregations began to dwindle long before the Blitz as the population moved out to the suburbs, but they still have their loyal supporters or have been converted to other uses.

Christ Church, at the junction of Broad, Wine and Corn Streets, is just 200 years old, its construction on the site of a medieval church founded in 1153 having been started in 1786 by the eminent Bristol architect William Paty. Inside it is like a Wren church in white and gold, and the poet Southey, born in Wine Street, used to watch the quarter-boys strike the quarter hours on its tower. It is now used as a centre for religious education.

30 shows the church *c.* 1938. Note the curved corner building in front of it, dominated by a huge neon sign 'Player's Please'.

31 shows the view today, the bells struck by the quarter-jacks, loaned to the church by the Corporation for 12½p a year (now 13p), being clearly visible above the 1883 portal designed by the Bristol architect Henry Williams.

32 shows the setting of the church from the northwest looking along Broad Street; the Lord Mayor's resplendent Daimler limousine in the foreground is parked on a double yellow line!

33

33 and **34** Yet another city centre church, this one is dedicated to All Saints in Corn Street. The original foundation was Norman, and indeed the two west bays are of that period. There was a great fire in 1466 that destroyed the city's reference library and after which the church was rebuilt. Another rebuilding took place in Queen Anne's time (1711-12), the architect being William Paul, to be completed five years later by George Townesend of London. The great tower had its lantern rebuilt in 1807 by Luke Henwood, and the long chancel itself was rebuilt in 1850.

This church, about which Keith Brace writes 'is dark haunting and no doubt haunted', has Rysbraek's sculptural monument of 1729 to Bristol's notable, Edward Colston (died 1721) who made much money from the slave trade.

33 shows the church in a street beset by moving or parked vehicles. From the blacked-out headlamp of the 1938 Rover car, it must have been taken during World War II.

Today the traffic has been banished and the whole prospect made infinitely more attractive (**34**).

34

35

36

35 shows the Lewins Mead Meeting, a Unitarian chapel, designed by (probably William) Blackburne of London *c.* 1786, and completed in 1791. It is of stone, with a five-bay front, pediment, and rusticated ground floor. Inside there was a handsome pulpit and, unusually, a coffered ceiling suspended from the roof by chains. It marks the beginning of the non-conformist takeover from the Anglican domination of the city centre. Note the 'nightmare hat stand' in the forecourt, a one-time noble plane tree desecrated in the way that is still so beloved by the British.

36 It was good to see in November 1986 that the old chapel has been refurbished and is now available for a new use.

37

37, 38 and **39** Bristol Bridge is where the city started, for it was at this point that the Avon was crossed (indeed the original name – Bricgstow – means 'the place of the bridge'). The first timber bridge was replaced by one of stone with four arches in 1247, and on it was built, in the fourteenth century, a chapel of Our Lady with a tower 100 ft (30 m) high.

Growing traffic caused the demolition of this bridge when it was over 500 years old, and a new stone structure of three arches was designed in 1764 by James Bridges, the work being executed by Thomas Paty, designer of the Public Library in 1740 and the Theatre Royal in 1766. The bridge was then widened in 1861.

37 is taken from a colour postcard, printed in Germany, and since it shows horse-drawn trams it must be pre-1895. All traffic is horse-drawn. To the left of centre is the church of St Nicholas in High Street, a remarkable Georgian Gothic building designed in 1763 by James Bridges, who came from North America, and continued afterwards by Thomas Paty. Higher up the street to the right is the spire of Christ Church, and on the right-hand side of the picture is the spirelet at the top of the tower of the Church of St Mary-le-Port.

38 show the southwest side of the bridge today, and just visible behind its superstructure are the Georgian stone arches. In the centre of the picture is the now prominent tower of St Mary-le-Port, the church gutted in the Blitz.

39 shows the deck of the bridge with the Church of St Nicholas, now used as a museum of local history and church art. Its tower clock is unique in having a second hand. Here the curfew is still rung at 9 pm. To the right of centre is the lantern tower of All Saints, and to the right again, the spire of Christ Church.

38

39

40 and **41** At the beginning of the reign of King William IV, Charles Dyer (1794-1848), the son of a Bristol surgeon, who was trained by the London architect William Brooks, was commissioned to design a grand new public building for the people of Clifton; the design was exhibited at the Royal Academy in 1832. Construction was delayed, and when the building was opened in 1840 it was rather inevitably called the Victoria Rooms.

It is a splendid Greek Revival building with a portico of eight columns, a rich entablature, and a pediment decorated with the sculpture of Jabez Tyley, whose Bristol workshops produced church monuments that can be seen all over Somerset. Here he has depicted the goddess Minerva in a chariot drawn by Apollo. Cliftonians used this building for concerts and play readings; Dickens gave readings here in the late 1860s, as did Oscar Wilde later on.

40 shows this monumental building in *c.* 1914 – in front of it a large, baroque, early twentieth-century fountain with weird sea creatures in the basins, and a statue of King Edward VII in Garter robes set up in 1912. The sculptor was Henry Poole. On the right-hand side of the photograph is a figure of a soldier of the Gloucester Regiment, a memorial of the Boer War. Note the ladies in the foreground – all in solemn black.

41

42

43

41 shows this scene in 1986, the main façade having just been refurbished. The regulation of modern traffic has resulted in a new traffic island on which the soldier and his bayonet are in less danger of destruction by a juggernaut. The Victoria Rooms have long been used by the University.

42, 43, 44 and **45** Here is College Green, 3 acres (1.2 ha) of open space in front of the Council House that have been a popular place for centuries. Tradition has it that St Augustine met leaders of the Celtic church of Britain here at the end of the sixth century. The name 'College' comes from the College of St Augustine, and the great abbey of that name, founded in 1142, that became Bristol Cathedral just four centuries later when Bristol was given cathedral rank under the provision of the Six Articles. These established, *inter alia*, the new dioceses of Bristol, Chester and Peterborough, hence the survival of their great Abbey churches.

42 shows the northeast sector of the Green *c.* 1935, the roadway running up to the foot of Park Street. On the left-hand side of the picture is Boehm's statue of Queen Victoria, commissioned at her Golden Jubilee in 1887, and to its right can be seen the top of the Cabot Tower. To the right of the photo is a fascinating fin-de-siècle building, the Cabot Cafe, part of the Cadena empire, with much art nouveau detail on the façade. It was designed by La Tribe and Weston in 1904 and must have played a significant part in Bristol's social life.

43 shows the same scene today. The tramlines have gone, the great elms were felled in 1950, and behind the new planting is the eastern section of the Council House, with golden unicorns on its roof. The statue of Queen Victoria has been moved to a more prominent place, and, sadly, the Cabot Café has gone, although the building still exists, just off the right of the photograph, and an example of undistinguished modernity has been built next to it.

44 is a gloomy Victorian photo of Bristol Cathedral in 1890, taken from the southeast, when church structures were expected to be shrouded with masses of ivy; this is contrasted with **45**, taken about half a century later. (*See also* **26**).

44

45

46

47

46 and **47** In 1862, Anglican churches in Clifton *reserved* most of their pews for those who could afford a pew rent – thus leaving little space available for the poor. A committee was set up to provide a new church without these rents, and the Vicar of the 1841 Church of St John the Evangelist in Clifton gave up a small part of his parish so that a site could be found and a new parish started.

The very distinguished Victorian architect Sir George Street (1824-81) designed the building, of which the chancel was consecrated on 8 June 1868 and the nave followed in 1872, dedicated to All Saints. A narthex was built in 1909 to a design by George Bodley (1827-1907), and a tower with a Flemish lantern, together with a sacristy, in 1928 by F.C. Eden. This splendid building, shown in **46**, incorporated the finest work of three notable architects, and it maintained the best of Catholic worship and practice from the beginning.

Most of this was to be destroyed in the Nazi holocaust when on 2 December 1940 a hail of incendiary bombs fired the church, and only the narthex and sacristy were left. About this destruction, Sir Nikolaus Pevsner wrote: 'That this church was gutted in the Second World War is a major loss to Victorian architecture. All Saints was a mature work of a serious and self-confident architect.'

A decision was reached *c.* 1962 to rebuilt the church, and Robert Potter FRIBA, FSA of Southampton was commissioned to design it. **47** shows this splendid new church that incorporates the narthex, the lower part of the 1868 tower, and the 1928 sacristy. The apex of the spire, which is made of laminated timber covered with aluminium, is 138 ft (42 m) from the ground.

The picture also shows the Great War Memorial Calvary, also designed by F.C. Eden, whilst inside the church, near the organ, is Eden's Calvary rescued by Clifton College scholars from the burning church that December night in 1940.

48

49

50

48 shows The Centre as it was 100 years ago. In the foreground is the Floating Harbour created by quaying an arm of the River Frome. The upper section beyond the drawbridge was filled in 1892. On the left side is an advertisement for 'Husband's Optician' and in the street below is a horse tram, the lines of which, clearly visible in the foreground, were laid down in 1875. Above the tram is the Roman Catholic church of St Mary-on-the-Quay, orginally designed for the Irvingites by the City Surveyor, Richard Pope, in 1839. Right of centre is the tower of St Stephen's Church.

49 is approximately the same view in 1902. The new electric trams had started seven years earlier with their elaborate street standards carrying the overhead cables. The tram in the foreground is bound for Hotwells. Note the roof-top advertisement hoardings of the shops on the left side of the road. There is a new bridge, and the dock warehouse(?) in the earlier picture has disappeared.

The open-topped trams clanged brusquely around the Tramways Centre, as it had become known, their blue sparks flashing at night; and in *its* centre was the place where the city's domestic servants met their beaux, known as Skivvies Island.

50, completing the trilogy, shows the Centre in 1985 – a very different scene. The northern part of the dock was filled in in 1939, and is now a large municipal flower bed.

The white stucco buildings on the west side have survived, but the noble tower of St Stephen's is being gradually crowded in. Pevsner says of this tower 'Large and proud with a Gloucester crown'. It was built *c.* 1450 and paid for by the Mayor John Shipward. The church itself is an archive of the city's history.

51, 52, 53 and **54** Following the Cabot voyage of 1497, the Society of Merchant Venturers of Bristol was given its Charter by Edward VI in 1552. Ships sailed out of the port of Bristol to all parts of the earth, and in the official guide to Bristol of 1929 there is an advertisement under the title 'Port of Bristol Liner Services' with no less than 120 ports served by liners departing from its docks. They range from Cork and Charleston to Torquay and Vera Cruz, and all places in between. In that year, 900 *million* bananas entered the port, 26 per cent of all imported tobacco, and over 10 per cent of all grain. But by 1971, the city docks had only 18 berths, and that had dwindled to 12 a year later. Keith Brace wrote that year 'the whole dock complex is moving back into the world of industrial archaeology'. Now Bristol has, sadly, travelled virtually the same road as Liverpool and London.

51 shows the hive of activity at the Baltic Wharf in the City Docks in 1931, with the unloading of Scandinavian timber from a steamship into the yards of May and Hassell Ltd. Note the horse on the right-hand sector of the picture, patiently waiting for work. The wharf was once the heart of Bristol's dockland; now it is a housing scheme.

51

52

52, in complete contrast, shows a bows-on view of the first propellor-driven ship in the world, the steamship *Great Britain*, in August 1985 at Gas Ferry Wharf, just upstream of the previous picture. This remarkable ship was designed by Isambard Kingdom Brunel in 1838 and the keel laid in July 1839. She was built in Wapping Dock at Bristol, from which the launch took place four years later. She was the largest ship in the world at 3440 tons.

53 is a link with Cabot's time, for it shows the replica of Drake's *Golden Hind* in the Floating Harbour. She was built about 1972.

54 is the fine bronze statue of Brunel outside the Bristol and West Building Society's headquarters at Broad Quay. The sculptor was the internationally known John Doubleday who was commissioned by the Society.

54

55 shows the main front of Bristol Temple Meads Station, taken about 60 years ago, with its intricate canopy and 100 ft (30 m) clock tower. The architects were Sir Matthew Digby Wyatt and Francis Fox. This new station was opened on 1 January 1878. Note the three elderly taxis left of centre, and, on the extreme right, two GWR horse-drawn delivery carts outside the parcels office. On the extreme left is a motor van belonging to the LMSR, this being a joint station, and nearby the Midland parcels and telegraph office.

There is a plaque in this station to the memory of Emily Saunders of Bristol, who gave so much of her life to the welfare of railwaymen. Towards the end of her life, they gave her a resplendent armchair for her comfort.

56 shows the station in 1986; on the left is the original western terminal of the Great Western Railway designed by Brunel, opened on 31 August 1840. It is being magnificently restored by the Brunel Engineering Centre Trust, whose object is to restore the station, a Grade 1 listed building, to provide a new engineering exhibition centre. It was last used as a railway station in September 1965.

The building to the right of the station with a corrugated asbestos roof was where trams came in on a spur from the main road in Bath Parade, so that passengers could alight and enter the station directly.

56 Over the parapet of the bridge visible in the photograph, now the main entrance to the old station, can be seen the last surviving rails of the tramway system last used in 1940. Note that the spire above the clock tower has gone – a victim of the Blitz.

55

56

57

58

57 and **58** Sir Felix Pole, General Manager of the GWR in the 1920s, wanted the railway to have the most powerful locomotive in Britain, and his chief mechanical engineer, Charles Collett, was to design and Swindon to produce, in July 1927, the first six engines to be known as *The Kings*, No. 6000, King George V, being No. 1. In all 30 of them were built between 1927-30, and they were the flagship of the line, the largest 4-6-0s on British metals.

57 shows No. 6011, King James I, built in April 1928, running into Temple Meads with a West of England train in July 1936.

Only three of the engines remain today. No. 6000, King George V, No. 6021, King Edward I, saved from the scrapheap in 1973 and now being restored by the Quainton Railway Society (founded 1969) at their centre 6 miles (9.5 km) northwest of Aylesbury; and No. 6023, King Edward II, built at Swindon in June 1930 that went to the great scrapyard at Barry in South Wales 32 years later. On 30 Decemer 1984, the remains of this engine arrived by road in Bristol, rescued by Harveys of Bristol to mark the 150th anniversary of the GWR. Here, in **58**, is this last ever giant in the old Fish Dock at Temple Meads awaiting restoration.

BATH

Then and Now

'Oldest bath runs out after 1,900 years.' So ran a *Times* headline on 3 December 1976, regarding the closure that day of the Hot Springs Treatment Centre at Bath, because of the withdrawal of National Health Service patients who formed 95 per cent of the clientèle. This city has attracted peoples from all over the world for almost 20 centuries for one reason: water. Half-a-million gallons every 24 hours gush from a spring at about 120°F (49°C), and according to a recent report, this water fell as rain perhaps 100,000 years ago. Those Health Service patients were given hydro-therapy in mineral water fortified with magnesium and sodium chloride, and calcium and sodium sulphate.

Bath has been known for these healing waters for about 3000 years, that is from the Bronze Age, long before the Romans established their spa. The district is rich in camps and earthworks, such as the great Celtic chamber-tomb at Stony Littleton, 5 miles (8 km) southwest of Bath near Camerton; Sul, the tutelary goddess of the springs, was created by the local Celts. She is not found anywhere else in the Roman Empire.

Although there had been Roman incursions into southern Britain from Gaul for a century between 55 BC and AD 43, the general invasion and Conquest began in the latter year with 22,000 troops from the II, IX, XIV and XX Legions, accompanied by about 18,000 auxiliaries, landing at Richborough near Sandwich in East Kent. It was the second Legion under Vespasian who advanced westwards, possibly as far as Devon. When Ostorius became the governor of the new territory in AD 47, he drew a frontier line, the Fosse Way, from Seaton on the Devon coast via Bath, Cirencester, Leicester to Lincoln.

Gold, silver, lead and tin had been mined in Britain by the Celts, who were skilled metallurgists (for example, tin was smelted in Cornwall *c.* 400 BC), and the Romans lost no time in exploiting the lead and silver ores of the Mendips, as well as the coal deposits in the Radstock area. The men of the XX Legion discovered at Bath the healing springs and the cult of Sul, and since bathing was a way of life to them, these new-found waters must have proved a godsend, especially to those who had lived in a far warmer climate. And so there was built a new Roman city covering 23 acres (9 ha), and its *raison d'être* was the spa, dominated by a fine temple dedicated to Minerva, equating her with Sul, the Celtic goddess. The Roman city spa was named Aquae Sulis; it shared with Buxton in Derbyshire – Aquae Arnemetiae – the distinction of being one of the leading therapeutic establishments in the western Empire, a place to which patients suffering from rheumatism and allied diseases came from Britain and northern Europe.

The commander of the province of Britain between AD 78-85, Julius Agricola, used a subtle technique in enervating the morale of conquered Britons. His son-in-law, Tacitus, the contemporary historian, writes 'They [the Britons] were lured to the blandishments of the baths and their luxurious feasts, and an unsophisticated people learnt to mistake the path of servitude for the highroad to culture.'

Aquae Sulis fits perfectly into this picture: its great bath, lined with lead from local mines, and the local coal supplying the perpetual fire in the temple of Sulis Minerva; visitors seeking refuge from the cold in this sheltered valley, seeking a sovereign remedy in the hot springs. The votive inscriptions in the museum indicate that patients journeyed from near and far to this spa – a town councillor from nearby Glevum (Gloucester); a sculptor from Corinium Dobunorum (Cirencester); professional men seeking a health-cure; and those from the mainland of Europe, from the Roman city of Trèves (Trier) just inside what is now the frontier of West Germany with Luxembourg; from Metz in Lorraine, and from Chartres. And the local freestone that the Romans used for their buildings was so useful that it has been found in buildings in Hereford, London and even in Suffolk.

This Roman city spa, with its baths, the temple, shops, houses and forum, or market place, flourished for 350 years. S.E. Winbolt writes

> Their citizens lived comfortably . . . their gabled houses were detached . . . they imported Italian sculpture, Italian craftsmen laid mosaic floors, and painted wall frescoes. They enjoyed imports from Gaul, Germany, and Italy – wine, oil, earthenware, bronze and glass goods. The forum, a market place with its adjuncts of shops, was a centre of civic life and government combining the functions of market, town-hall, law courts, exchange, and a gathering place. (*Britain under the Romans, 1945*)

The departure of Constantine III from Britain in the year 407 marked the end of Roman power in Britain. One of his generals, Gerontius, a Briton, who believed himself to be slighted by Constantine, invited the Germans to invade Britain in 409, and the Roman-Britons were left almost defenceless. By the middle of that century, rule was passing to the Angles and Saxons, and the great Roman civilization was destroyed. The spa and the baths now faced abandonment and an uncertain future.

It seems that the onset of the Saxons may have signified the end, although Ralph Whitlock's book *Somerset* (Batsford 1975) considers that the spa continued to be used for another century. The *Anglo-Saxon Chronicle* throws a glimmer of light on this with a brief reference in the year 577 – 'This year Cuthwin and Ceawlin fought with the Britons on the spot that is called Erham, and took from them three cities, Gloucester, Cirencester and *Bath*'. Erham is the present-day Dyrham, 6 miles (9.5 km) due north of Bath, and it is noteworthy that all these 'cities' formed a Roman settlement. If the chronicler is right, then Bath was not abandoned entirely, and a century later the Abbess Bertana established a convent there, and St Aldhelm consecrated a church at Akemancester (Bath) to St Michael circa the year 700. (Aldhelm, a relative of King Ina, founder of Wells, became Abbot of Malmesbury in 675 and first bishop of Sherborne.) This Saxon name for Bath – Akemancester – is interesting, for on the map of the Roman roads in Britain, Akeman Street was the highway that led northeastwards from Corinium (Cirencester) across the South Midlands for 40 miles (64 km) to the Roman settlement of Bicester in Oxfordshire. And it is used again in the *Anglo-Saxon Chronicle* – 'AD 973. Here was Edgar of Angles lord, with courtly pomp hallow'd to king at Akemancester, the ancient city, whose modern sons dwelling therein, have named her BATH'. This does not give the impression that the settlement had been entirely abandoned.

This hallowing of Edgar was in fact the Coronation, carried out with great solemnity at Bath on Pentecost, 11 May 973, with the assent of the Pope, by both Primates Dunstan and Oswald in the presence of the national parliament, the Witenagemot. Although Edgar had become king in 959 at the age of 16, under a firm administration the country enjoyed peace, and when he died on 8 July 975, he was called Edgar the Peaceful.

A church served by secular canons, as in Wells, was recorded in Bath in 781. Dunstan made it monastic when the Benedictines from Ghent arrived, and Edgar was crowned in their abbey church. Soon after this, St Aelphege became abbot; and a century later, in 1088, when John de Villula became bishop of Wells, and removed the see to Bath, he resided here nominally as abbot, the former abbot becoming a prior, so that Bath Abbey is in fact a misnomer. John commenced to built a Norman church but much of the city was destroyed in a great fire in 1137, and the splendid church of today was not started until 1499 by bishop King. The monastery had on average about 22 monks, small compared with Glastonbury or Bury St Edmunds, and when it was surrendered on 27 January 1539, the deed was signed by the prior William Holloway, the sub-prior, the prior of Dunster and 18 monks. Holloway received a pension of £80 a year, a very large income for the sixteenth century, and the others smaller amounts depending on seniority.

Soon afterwards the church was stripped of its glass, its lead and its bells, and what was left – a skeleton of a church – was sold by the king to Humphrey Colles, who in turn sold it to Matthew Colthurst, whose son presented it to the citizens in 1560. Seventeen years earlier, Parliament had passed an act making the dean and chapter of Wells the sole chapter for the see. The church, however, was in a parlous state, so much so that Queen Elizabeth issued letters patent *c.* 1575, authorising collections for the rebuilding of the church in Bath to be made for seven years *in every part of the kingdom*. A reconsecration took place in 1590, when it was dedicated to ss Peter and Paul, and the Queen gave the town a Charter; then under Bishop Montague (1608-16) a thorough restoration took place. Although Celia Fiennes recorded on a visit to Bath in 1695 that 'much company walked in the church in wet weather', the nave was not, in fact, vaulted until 1869.

In 1616, the Queen of James I, Anne of Denmark, came to partake of the healing waters – a visit which may have been a turning point in Bath's history. This regal visit was followed by other noble and aristocratic visitors, and in the reign of Charles II, in 1677, an attempt was made in the springs to find a remedy for the sterility of the Queen, Catherine of Braganza. It was not realized, and her husband found solace elsewhere! But royal visits increased: James II and his Queen Mary in 1681, Princess Anne the following year, and as Queen in 1702-3.

Thus the scene was set for Georgian Bath, heralded by the arrival in 1705 of the Welshman, Richard Nash, born in 1674 in Swansea, his Pembrokeshire father being a partner in a glass works. He had been educated at Carmarthen School, and sent, like so many of his countrymen, to Jesus College, Oxford, founded in June 1571 as a place of higher education for Welsh students. Pevsner says of him – 'failed at University, failed at the Temple, failed in the Army and then succeeded in making a living out of gambling'.

Nash went to Bath following the success of Queen Anne's visit, and had he not become its Master of Ceremonies, the greatness of eighteenth-century Bath might not have ensued. The spa had been visited for health reasons; he made it into a great social centre, and, using a rule book, enforced by dictatorship, taught it elegance! He became known as 'Beau', though not at all a beau, being of harsh countenance.

Just as the beginnings of Bath had originated with the cult of the Celtic goddess Sul, so its meteoric rise to becoming the Queen of British Spas was entirely due to three Brythonic Celts – Nash from west Wales, William Oliver from Ludgvan in southwest Cornwall, and Ralph Allen from St Blazey in mid-Cornwall.

Up to 1725, the buildings of Bath had followed Bristol fashion. The change was due not only to Nash, Allen and Oliver, but to the architects John Wood, and his son, also John. From about 1715 onwards, Bath became as fashionable as London. The nobility and the aristocracy flocked to London for the season between May and July, and then spent the remainder of the summer at a spa town, and above all at Bath. Ralph Allen, the entrepreneur, provided the material to erect the new buildings when he purchased the stone quarries at Combe Down. By his ability in promoting the quality of Bathstone, he made it acceptable and then famous. Wood and Nash worked for precisely the same ideals – discipline in building and discipline in manners. In his *English Social History* (1942) G.M. Trevelyan writes

> Beau Nash employed his despotic power to compel the fashionable world to lay aside their swords when they entered his domain and in this he did as good service to the community as in teaching the country bumpkins to discard their top boots and coarse language at the evening assemblies . . . but he encouraged public gambling and took for himself a percentage on the winnings of the bank.

John Wood and other architects built so much of Georgian Bath as lodgings for letting in the season, and the Cornish physician Dr William Oliver came to live there in 1725, to become the physician *par excellence* in this queen of the spas. He is remarkable in the history of Bath as one who never forgot the plight of those less fortunate. He found expression for this in the founding of the then General Hospital, afterwards the Royal Mineral Water Hospital, designed by the elder Wood and built in 1737-42; he was appointed physician to the hospital in 1740. He represents the best of Bath, as contrasted with the frivolous age of Nash, where the steady work of healing and amelioration was carried on, in the same way that the Romans had done centuries before. His very name has descended to us in the famous Bath Oliver digestive biscuit, which he invented just before he died, entrusting the recipe to his coachman Atkins, who afterwards opened a shop in Green Street and made a fortune!

Edith Jolly in *The New Bath Guide* says

> Doing the Bath season meant spending every moment of the day seeing and being seen. One visited the Cross and the King's or the Queen's Bath (ladies only), or the Pump Room to drink the waters before 10 a.m. Opinions differed as to the flavour: some said it was like a rare Beaune wine; others, that it tasted more like warm flat-irons.

Breakfast was at 10 o'clock and the main meal of the day between 2 and 3 o'clock in the afternoon. So much wine was drunk, and heavy meals eaten that there was every inducement to take the waters! Tea was at 5 o'clock, and the evenings spent at a concert, theatre or ball. The *beau monde* flocked to Bath, certain that dignity would prevail, and the city became the rallying point of fashion and society during its season.

But, inevitably, the Beau's influence waned. Firstly, Parliament legislated against gambling between 1739-45, and in his old age he was vexed by lawsuits and by slanders. His fortunes declined and he died aged 87, in comparative poverty, on 12 February 1761 in St John's Court. He had been a generous man, protecting young men and maidens from falling victims to charlatans. The citizens gave him a handsome funeral and in the 'Abbey' church there is a fitting monument with an inscription in Latin. It says of him 'Elegantiae Arbiter' – an Arbiter of Elegance, commemorated on the walls of a Benedictine priory.

John Wood the Elder had died in 1754, Ralph Allen and Dr Oliver a decade later, and Bath changed. Nash's organising genius made the spa both popular and fashionable, and it was this very popularity that was the cause of its gradual decline. The privileged aristocratic society left and a different class replaced it. Social climbers came instead, and, later on, what had been the lodgings for the season were sold as permanent homes for retired army officers and the clergy. But there was an Indian summer in this latter part of the eighteenth century, and Bath's praises were sung in both prose and verse. Thus Bath became the city of Smollett and Sheridan.

Tobias Smollett, born at Bonhill House near Loch Lomond in 1721, became a doctor by profession, who turned in writing in 1746, and was a frequent visitor to Bath, using his medical knowledge to write in 1752 *Essay on the External Use of Water with particular Remarks on the Mineral Waters of Bath*. But earlier he had written *Roderick Random* and *Peregrine Pickle* illustrating all the vices, intrigues and corruptions of Bath society. They are, in effect, a Plain Man's Guide to Eighteenth-Century Wickedness. It is small wonder that in a dictionary of biography (1885) one reads 'His writings are not fit for delicate hands to touch by reason of their indecency'. All this wickedness was confirmed in a report in *The Times* of 8 September 1986 under the heading 'Bath, sin city of the west, is exposed.' In it, Dr Graham Davis, a Bath historian, revealed how he had spent months examining old police records that proved the existence of brothels all over the city, gambling on a large scale and horrific crimes of violence in the streets. The most famous Madame was Oliva Poole, and people came from far and wide to enjoy Bath's illicit attractions.

Smollett acquired serenity only in the last years of his life – he died in 1771 – and in his most mature work, *Humphrey Clinker*, written that year, he gives an authentic picture of Bath that followed the age of Nash. R.A. Lendon Smith wrote in *Bath* (Batsford 1944) of 'a busy jostling crowd of high-born and low-born all engaged in a frantic round of pleasure and diversion, an easy prey to sharks and fortune-hunters'.

The modern theatre in Bath dates from about 1710 when one was built in Trim Street, soon to be replaced by a second in Orchard Street, now the Masonic Hall. It became such an important asset to Bath that George III granted a Royal Patent in 1768 and thereafter it became the Theatre Royal. A new theatre became necessary at the turn of the century and this was built in 1805 near Beauford Square, incorporating part of Nash's first house. The architect was George Dance the Younger, and then after a fire in 1863, the interior was remodelled by the Bath theatre architect, C.J. Phipps (1835-97). It has now been dramatically restored with a complete facelift, inside and out.

On to the Bath scene in 1770 came Thomas Sheridan, the Irish actor and compiler of an English dictionary. His third son, Richard Brinsley, born in Dublin in 1751, was the author of *The Rivals* (1775), followed by *The Duenna* and *School for Scandal* (conceived in Bath in the 1750s, and first performed at Covent Garden in 1755). One of the classic love-affairs of the eighteenth century was that of Richard and the beautiful Elizabeth Linley, splendid singer and daughter of Thomas Linley, who played an important part in Bath's musical establishment. Thomas had planned that she should marry a rich Wiltshire landowner named Long, and indeed the marriage was arranged. But the girl asserted her independence (quite novel in Georgian England) and secured her release from him. A dissipated army officer, Major Matthews, then sought her favours, but Elizabeth rejected him also, and she and Sheridan eloped from No. 11 Royal Crescent, and were wed in a Normandy village.

The clientèle of the spa may have changed after 1765, but splendid buildings continued to be erected: the Royal Crescent (1767-74), Camden Crescent (1788), Lansdown Crescent (1789-92), St. James's Square (1793), Somerset Place (1793), and Cavendish Crescent, completed as late as 1830. Pevsner remarks 'As a piece of town planning, Georgian Bath is unique in England and indeed in Europe'.

The pivots of the social life of Bath since early in the eighteenth-century have been the Pump Room and the Assembly Rooms. The original Pump Room was used purely for medical purposes and had been built by Nash in 1706. Over the next 80 years it was greatly enlarged. The crowds who came to Bath in the 1780s, the age of Sheridan, found the Pump Room too small, and the City Architect Thomas Baldwin submitted to the Corporation a comprehensive plan for rebuilding the whole area. It was finally completed in 1799 by his successor, John Palmer, after a bitter disagreement between the councillors and Baldwin over design details. The Greek inscription on the pediment reads ARISTON MEN HYDOR – 'Water is best'.

There have been several sets of Assembly Rooms in Bath over a long period, but those of today in Bennett and Alford Streets, east of The Circus, were designed by John Wood the Younger in 1796, and completed two years later. The noble building had four main rooms: the great Ball Room (at the time it was built the largest room in the city); the Octagon Room, used for cards; the Card Room, after the Octagon was too small; and the Tea Room.

In its heyday, there could have been 1000 people in this building, dancing, tea-drinking and card-playing; balls were held twice a week, occasionally masked. The Prince of Wales attended a great ball in 1796.

After Bath had ceased to be the queen of the resorts, when the new railways made the Alps, the English Lakes and the Highlands accessible to international travellers, the Assembly Rooms became a concert hall for orchestras and recitalists. Franz Liszt came, as did Johann Strauss the Elder, and Sir Arthur Sullivan. Charles Dickens too gave readings from his works (1867-9), and in World War I the Ball Room became a cinema. By 1931, however, it had deteriorated greatly.

In those days, without the benefit of legislation to protect historic buildings, such a dilapidated building might well have been demolished, perhaps to become a site for a purpose-built cinema. But help came through the Society for the Protection of Ancient Buildings, founded in 1877 by William Morris, when the Rooms were purchased by the late Ernest Cook (of the Thomas Cook family – pioneers in travel), who presented them to the National Trust in 1931. The Trust restored them and then leased them to the Corporation in 1938. That October, there was a brilliant social gathering, rivalling the great days of Beau Nash, when Marina, Duchess of Kent, danced at the re-opening 'in the presence of a throng of delighted people. The fashions and dances of the eighteenth-century were sedulously rehearsed by the company. All was gaiety and mirth' (R.A.L. Smith: *Bath*).

Three and a half years later, on the evening of 25 April 1942, the sirens sounded and a savage aerial bombardment started before midnight; after a short lull it was followed by a second, and less than 24 hours later, by another even more deadly. The Luftwaffe bombers roared down as low as 50 ft (15 m) and fired on the streets and buildings of Bath. The Assembly Rooms were so ruined that only the outer walls remained.

The eminent figure entrusted to restore them to their classical glory, perhaps the greatest architect of his generation skilled in these matters, was the late Sir Albert Richardson of Ampthill, RA, FRIBA, President of the Royal Academy 1954. But it was not until 1963 that the Trust was able to restore the building for the second time to its former glory and original purposes. The magnificent 1771 chandeliers sparkle in their original positions, and yet the Rooms are not a museum, except for the Museum of Costume established by Doris Langley Moore in the basement. They are available for antique fairs, concerts, university celebrations and even tea-dances.

At the first national census in 1801, Bath had a population of 30,000 and was ninth in the list of English cities in order of population. It had been rebuilt in a style befitting the solid splendour of that age, and, to quote Peter Smithson (*Bath:* 1971) 'In its town organisation and in its architecture, Bath is like nowhere else. Ordinary day-to-day living in Bath was given the attention and love that elsewhere was devoted only to the glory of the state.'

Although the railway proper did not arrive until 1840, there had been a railway (of sorts) over a century earlier when Ralph Allen, who had bought the stone quarries on Combe Down in 1727, laid a 45 in (114 cm) gauge wooden railroad to convey Bathstone from the quarries down to the River Avon, after having been instrumental in effecting navigation of that river opened that year all the way from Bristol to Bath. The first Avon River Navigation Act had been passed in 1712. The earliest known railway print, drawn by Anthony Walker, in 1750, shows this Combe Down Railway alongside the stone wall bordering Prior Park, where there is a single line of timber rails. The rolling stock comprises flat trucks on four flanged wheels carrying blocks of newly-dressed freestone.

On 31 August 1840, the station at Bath of Brunel's Great Western Railway was opened, then the eastern terminus of the line from Bristol. As soon as the great Box Tunnel, 2212 yd (2022 m) in length, was completed, the line was opened from Bath to London on 30 June 1841. The census that year reveals a total population of 53,000 – thus the city had almost doubled since 1801.

On Michaelmas Day, in 1760, William Thomas Beckford was born, probably in London. He became an immensely rich genius, brought up at his father's Palladian (1768) mansion at Fonthill, 6 miles (9.5 km) northeast of Shaftesbury. In the 1790s, Beckford commissioned James Wyatt to build an enormous Gothick 'abbey' at Fonthill, and he moved into the still incomplete mansion in 1802. He lived there for 21 years, moving at the end of 1822 to Bath, after the completion of the abbey in 1812. He chose Bath because for him the city had the finest prospect in Europe. He had purchased Nos. 19/20 Lansdown Crescent, and his estate continued up through the garden and a plantation to his tower, the Lansdown Tower. In his old age, he would drive up to the tower, accompanied by his dogs and his servant, an Italian dwarf named Perro.

This extraordinary folly was designed for Beckford by Henry Goodridge (*c.* 1800-63) and built in 1825-6. It has been described architecturally as a mixture of Tuscan, Roman, Byzantine and Greek styles. Beckford kept his finest china on the ground floor and the Crimson Drawing Room and Etruscan Library were on the second. Today it is open to the public, and if one has the stamina to climb the 156 steps up to the Belvedere at the summit (154 ft [47 m]), on a fine day the Black Mountains in Gwent can be seen, 45 miles (72.5 km) away. There is also a small museum, and a chapel used for the Lansdown Cemetery where both the client and his architect are buried. William Beckford, author of the Gothic novel *Vathek* (1784), and builder of the greatest folly of all, Fonthill Abbey, achieved what is given to so few – he became a legend in his own lifetime, and the people of Bath viewed him with a mixture of fear, awe and wonderment. Fonthill, in southwest Wiltshire, was a large Gothick mansion, built in imitation of a vast medieval abbey at a cost of about £275,000, between 1795 and 1812, and had an octagonal tower about 230 ft (70 m) high. On 21 December 1825, the tower collapsed in an enormous cloud of rubble and dust, and slid into the fountain court. The ruins lay untouched until 1844, when Beckford died at Lansdown Crescent, and have today been described 'a comfortable ruin of Beckford's harum-scarum with its madly aspiring tower'.

The *New Bath Guide* (Eva Jolly, 1985) says

> Many of the best Georgian buildings were destroyed during the 'Baedeker' raids of the Second World War. What the bombs didn't quite reach, the arrogant 'town planners' ['town destroyers' would be a better word] of the 1950s and 1960s knocked down instead. The less said about their folly the better.

Forty years ago, the Corporation issued a decree that all building in Bath should be of Bathstone and consonant to the architectural style of the eighteenth century. Times have changed, however, and this decree was not observed. Writing in 1934, Maxwell Fraser recorded the beauty and *serenity* of Bath. Today, in these last years of the twentieth century, there seems to be a movement that is speaking out against the brutalism movement in architecture. Bath today is hardly serene – there is far too much motor traffic. In fact, 100 tourist coaches *per hour* in high season pass through Queen Square, creating so much detriment to fine buildings that their future looks threatened. Bath must consider if it can afford to endure the onslaught of mass tourism and still contemplate the future with calm.

Bath started with mineral springs, and so it was heartening to read in *The Times* on 15 January 1977 the headline 'Old Royal Baths at Spa to be reopened', and the report that plans had been announced the previous day to reopen the Baths, so restoring to the ancient spa its therapeutic waters in which people have been soaking their aches and pains since the hot mineral springs were named Aquae Sulis.

In March 1986, it was revealed that the Pump Room is Britain's second most popular tourist attraction, second only to the Tower of London. It was restored in 1984-6 at a cost of £80,000, and 1,000,000 visitors were expected in 1986.

1, taken in 1911, in a more leisurely age of horse-drawn vehicles, is of The Paragon. This elegant street was complete by 1768, and the person responsible for it was a Mr Thomas Atwood, rather delightfully described as 'a common-council man, banker and eminent plumber'. Each doorway is framed with Doric pilasters and pediment, and a similar pediment is found in the centre window on the first floor. Note the tramline and overhead electric cables.

2 is the same view 75 years later. The road is now part of the A4 trunk road (the London Road), and whilst taking this photograph I was almost knocked over by a car being driven along the *pavement* in order to park outside a house. Note how the vista is now closed completely by trees.

Jane Austen lived for a time at no. 1, and no. 33 was the home of the well-known Sarah Siddons (born Brecon 1755). She made her reputation as a great tragic actress in Bath before moving to Drury Lane in 1782. She was painted by Joshua Reynolds and by Gainsborough.

1

2

3

4 was taken from an upper storey at the rear of the Sally Lunn Refreshment house (*see* **8**). **3** was taken about a century ago.

Allen's chief claim to posterity was his patronage of a group of men who attended gatherings at Prior Park, among them Alexander Pope the poet, David Garrick the actor, Gainsborough the painter, and Pitt, Earl of Chatham. Allen died in 1764.

3 and **4** Ralph Allen, 'the man of Bath', was a Cornishman born to a publican near St Blazey Gate, St Austell in 1693. His grandmother was the Post-mistress at St Columb Major, and he started his career in that establishment. In 1709 he moved to Bath, there married a daughter of Marshal Wade and became Post-master for the city. He was blessed with gifts of ingenuity and enterprise, and used them to institute great reforms in the postal services, organising a system of cross-country mails, where previously everything had gone through London.

His mansion, Prior Park, 1½ miles (2.5 km) southeast of the city, was completed about 1750. It has been a Roman Catholic boys' school since 1830. He had a small town house built about 1728 of which Sir Nikolaus Pevsner says 'The façade is the most important and instructive document to show John Wood's style', when he came to Bath in 1727. It has a rusticated ground floor with arched entrance, giant Corinthian columns, and a richly decorated pediment. It is located at no. 2 Old Lilliput Alley and is extraordinarily difficult to photograph as it is hemmed in completely.

4

5

6

5 Queen Anne started the fashion for visiting Bath in 1702, and returned the following year. Immense crowds followed the sovereign, and John Harvey built the first Pump Room in 1706 at the behest of Richard 'Beau' Nash in his bid to make Bath the most fashionable city. Eighty years later, Thomas Baldwin, who had been appointed City Architect in 1776, started work on the present Pump Room.

The photograph, dated 1914, shows Baldwin's Colonnade (taken from an upper window of the Grand Pump Room Hotel, see 7) which was the first structure to be erected. Its pediment is decorated with a profile of the Greek goddess of health, Hygeia, flanked by a pair of sphinxes. Note at the left-hand side of a sphinx a municipal fire-hydrant plate – a jarring juxtaposition.

The main Pump Room was Baldwin's design, but a major disagreement with the Corporation led to him being dismissed in 1792, the building started in 1790 being completed by John Palmer in 1799. In front of the Pump Room was Stall Street with its tramline, and to the right of the building the big 1875 chimney of the Bath Steam Laundry.

6 shows the same scene today: Stall Street has become a traffic-free pedestrian precinct, and, in season, the Colonnade is festooned with gaily coloured flower baskets. Behind the pediment is the upper part of the medieval Abbey church.

7

8

7 and **8** are good illustrations of urban renewal. On a site on the west side of Stall Street, itself built on top of the Roman bath, and where a head of Minerva was found in 1727, there was a well-known hostelry, the White Hart Hotel. This was torn down in 1868, to be replaced by the Grand Pump Room Hotel, designed by a Bath architect who won the competition for it – William John Willcox. He was an early member of the RIBA, being elected an Associate (ARIBA) in 1863. Later he went into partnership with James Wilson FSA, architect of Cheltenham College. Willcox was practising at no. 1 Belmont in Bath at the time he produced the drawings for this grand hotel, with its French pavilion roofs, slightly reminiscent of St Ermyn's Hotel in Westminster. The photographer was standing on the roof of the loggia behind the Colonnade (see **5**) and part of the pediment coping is visible in the bottom left-hand corner.

The hotel opened in 1869, but suffered the fate of its predecessor 90 years later when the foundation stone was laid for Arlington House, seen in **8**.

11 shows the Abbey precinct crammed with tourists in 1985 high season.

9

9, **10** and **11** show the west front of the Abbey Church of SS Peter and Paul, one of the last big Perpendicular monastic churches to be built. Oliver King, Bishop of Bath and Wells, visited the priory in 1499, and found it in a state of moral decay and the church in great need of reconstruction. Together with the then Prior, William Bird, the new building designed by William and Robert Vertue rose out of the old one but was still incomplete at the time of the Dissolution in 1539. In 1572 it became the mother church of Bath, but the nave was not roofed until 1614; Sir Gilbert Scott completely restored the building between 1864-73. Bishop King had the representation of his vision of the Trinity carved on the West Front, with angels ascending and descending ladders, clearly visible in **10**, taken *c.* 1927. Note the Bath Chairs.

9 is dated *c.* 1890, and to the right of the Abbey is an interesting Georgian building operated as the premises of the Bible and Religious Tract Societies. In the second photograph (**10**) this building has been replaced by a new one, designed by John M. Brydon in 1897. He was the architect for the 1895 extension to Bath's Guildhall.

10

11

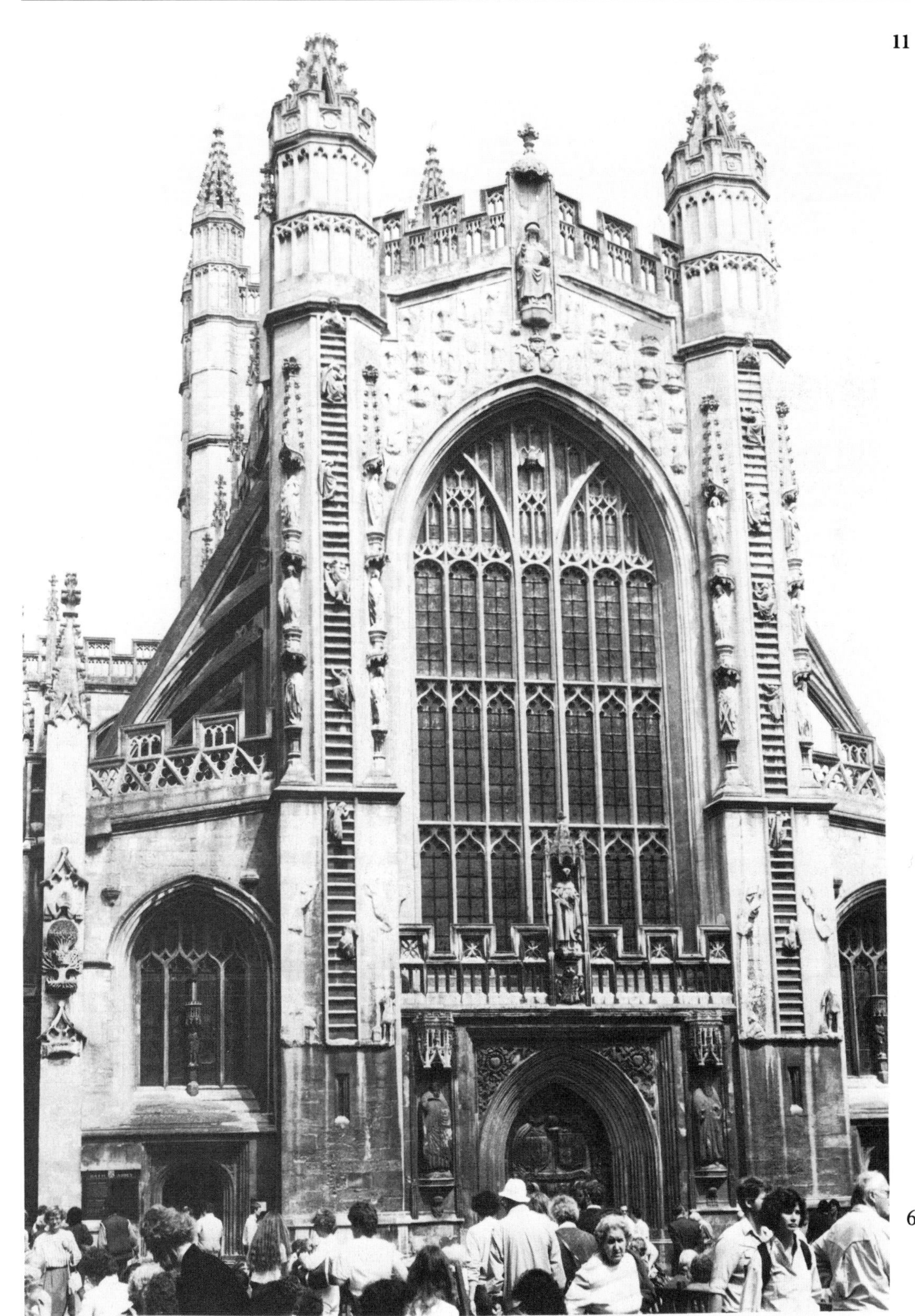

12

13

12 and **13** In front of the east end of the Abbey is Orange Grove, where Beau Nash erected an obelisk in 1734 inscribed to the Prince of Orange. From the northeast corner of the Grove there is a splendid view of the great church, its architecture so much akin to the Royal Chapels of King's at Cambridge and St George's, Windsor. We even know the names of the craftsmen (Edward Leycester and John Multon) who so lovingly created this part of the church in the days before the Dissolution on 27 January 1539.

The flying buttresses – stone engineering to support the upper part of the main walls – were inserted as late as 1835, when the first restoration scheme was undertaken by the architect George Manners of Bath (*c.* 1789-1866).

12 gives a delightful picture of Bath in the more leisurely days of *c.* 1930 when you could water your horse at a convenient drinking trough and park your Austin 6 without fear of a traffic warden. A tramline passed through the street.

13 shows the same view today; the traffic is continuous around the Orange Grove roundabout.

THE BATH & PORTLAND

15

14, 15, 16 and **17** This sequence of four photographs is centred on the great Roman Bath. The town was a centre of Roman life and has perhaps the finest Roman remains in northern Europe. The Romans called the town Aquae Sulis, after the Celtic goddess Sul, and the spa shared with Buxton (Aquae Arnemetiae) the title of leading establishment in therapeutics in the Western Empire, skilled in the treatment of rheumatic and allied diseases. Its reputation was international.

The Great Bath was paved with 15 in (38 cm) thick stone blocks, covered with 14 great sheets of local lead, still intact, mined at Charterhouse near Cheddar, the water gushing out at 120° (49°C) and cooling in the bath to 62°F (16°C). It measures 83 x 40 ft (25 x 12 m), tapering to 73 x 29 ft (22 x 9 m) at the bottom. The treatment was not unlike the present-day Turkish bath – cold room, warm room, sauna then the plunge into the warm pool.

Although the first evidence of the baths was discovered in 1755, the Great Bath was not found until 1880, and after this date the balustraded superstructure and statues of Roman emperors was built (**14**).

Adjacent to the south transept of the Abbey there is a very pleasant late Georgian building that once housed the offices of the Bath and Portland Stone Firms Ltd. About 1965 the firm decided to rebuild on the site and submitted a design for a new block by the architects Robert Matthew, Johnson-Marshall & Partners, shown in **15**. **16** shows the west elevation of the proposed building superimposed.

There was considerable feeling throughout Bath, and further afield, that the design was insensitive, and the City Council refused planning permission. One comment was that the proposal was 'a sin of the first magnitude'. A public inquiry was held and the Minister of Housing and Local Government dismissed the appeal.

The fourth photograph, **17**, shows the site today. The Stone Company's former offices are the City Council's Department of Environmental Services. Glazing bars have been inserted into nearly all of the windows and there have been sensitive alterations to the ground floor. Surely the Minister's decision has been vindicated?

16

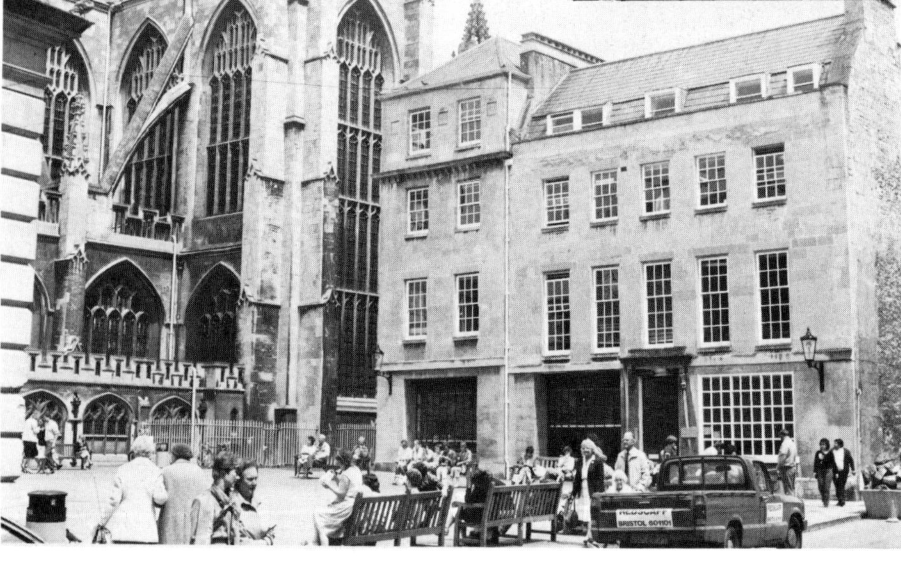

17

18

19

18 and **19** Milsom Street, the principal shopping street of the city, was named after Daniel Milsom, a wine cooper who leased the land from the Corporation in 1762; the layout is by John Wood the Elder. On the east side (centre left in **18**) is a group, now called Somerset Buildings, designed by the city architect, Thomas Baldwin, in 1782. He had been an assistant in the city architect's office and was appointed to the top post in 1776. The group was originally called Baldwin's Buildings, and had a rusticated ground floor with arched windows and doors, giant Corinthian columns through the first and second storeys, and the centre curved forward. Further down the street is no. 46, built in 1904, and behind is the former proprietary Octagon Chapel, designed by Thomas Lightholer in 1765. Its organist was the distinguished astronomer Sir William Herschel (born Hanover 1738: died 1822) who discovered the planet Uranus, and who also led the orchestra at the public rooms. The chapel is behind the Royal Photographic Society's shop and can be visited.

The street became fashionable as *the* shopping street – the east side known as the shilling side, the west the half-crown side – and a print of 1820 shows the shops with bowed fronts.

19 shows Milsom Street in 1985, and clearly visible is a traffic warden, apparently about to book a car parked on the double-yellow lines. The different fashions in the two photographs will bear closer inspection and comparison.

21

20 and 21 George Trim was a prosperous Bath clothier, and he began to build Trim Street in 1707, in which there are still three interesting houses: no. 2 of 1699, no. 5 of *c.* 1720, and no. 17 of 1724. The street adjoined and was just outside the medieval city wall.

No. 5 is shown on the right-hand side of **20** and is a splendid Palladian house of two storeys with rusticated angle pilasters, the doorway with fluted Ionic pilasters and curved pediment, whilst the centre window above has fluted Corinthian pilasters. At one time it belonged to the father of Major-General James Wolfe, Lieutenant General Edward Wolfe, and James frequently stayed there. On the day before he sailed for Canada (he was killed on the Heights of Abraham during the seige of Quebec, September 1759) he dined with Pitt the Elder, the Earl of Chatham, at no. 7 The Circus in Bath.

20 shows a cobbled street, with old-fashioned cottage loaves in the baker's shop window under the arch, and a youth in boots and a flat cap sitting on the steps. Horse dung litters the cobbles. The Wolfe House is dreary and has lost its glazing bars in the lower ground-floor sashes.

21, taken in 1985, shows that the cobbles and the bakery have gone, but no. 5 now has all its appropriate windows, resplendent with window boxes.

22

23

22 and **23** John Wood the Younger completed the building of The Circus after the death of his father in 1754, and then proceeded to build the Royal Crescent. This is a semi-elliptical terrace of 30 splendid houses over a sweep exceeding 500 ft (150 m), fronted originally by open fields but now by the lawn and fine trees of Victoria Park. It was completed in 1774. To quote Walter Ison – 'At once the finest building in Bath and the greatest single achievement in the whole field of urban architecture'. It is indeed a noble curve, dominated by Ionic columns through the first and second storeys.

At no. 11 lived the beautiful Elizabeth Linley who eloped with Richard Brinsley Sheridan, the playright, in 1772. Her father was Thomas Linley, the city's musical director, and their descendants today are the Earl of Snowdon and his children by Princess Margaret. Emma, Nelson's mistress, was a maid in the Linley household. Sir Isaac Pitman, the inventor of a system of shorthand, lived at no. 17. No. 1 Royal Crescent has been meticulously restored by the Bath Preservation Trust and is now a domestic museum.

The photographs show the cobbled paving of 1932 with an elderly limousine, horse-drawn cart and a delivery boy with his large wicker basket, contrasted with the scene today. The cobbles are still there but are inevitably littered with parked cars. The nineteenth-century lamp colums have survived, but many of the windows have had new sashes with glazing bars. It is to be regretted that not every window has been dealt with in a similar manner, despite the grants available from the Bath Preservation Trust.

24

25

24 and **25** Queen Square, Bath, reveals John Wood at his best. Following a training in London, Wood came to Bath in 1727, started the Square the following year and completed it about seven years later. The photographs show the grandest, north, side of the Square, named after Princess Caroline of Brandenburg, who married Prince George in 1705, and who ascended the throne in 1727. She lived for a time at 93 Sydney Street.

Here are seven large houses erected to provide superior accommodation for visitors. The centre of the block has six large Corinthian columns and a very large pediment surmounted by an urn. Nikolaus Pevsner says of it 'One of the grandest Palladian compositions in England designed before 1730'. John Wood himself lived in the centre at no. 24.

The south side is now the Hotel Francis that arose out of the wreck following the Nazi aerial bombardment of 1942. When the hotel was modernised in 1933, its boarding terms were 3½ guineas (£3.67) per *week*!

24 shows this splendid north side of the Square with a fascinating disc-wheel open tourer parked on the corner. The 1985 picture (**25**) reveals that the western end of the block has been invaded by creeper right up to the dormers, and only one house has its appropriate windows with glazing bars.

26

27

26 and **27** Leading northwards out of the northeastern corner of Queen Square is Gay Street, named after a Bath Surgeon, Robert Gay, who owned the land. It is the work of both the Woods.

26, taken in the 1920s, shows the corner of the Square and opposite it, no.41 Gay Street, built by Elder Wood for himself in 1740. It is a delightful piece of gay Baroque with intermittently blocked pairs of Ionic columns. The houses climb the hill from the corner. The 1985 photograph (**27**) reveals that the street is part of a major traffic route, but is still intact.

Amongst those who have lived in this street was the Italian musician, Venanzio Rauzzini, born in Camerino in 1746. He was a male soprano who came to London in 1774, and then to Bath in 1780, where he was the Director of Concerts for 30 years. He died in Bath in 1810. In addition, Josiah Wedgwood lived at no. 30 and William Friese-Green, the pioneer of cinematography, at no. 23. John Wood the Younger and Jane Austen also had homes here, Miss Austen's being one of five houses in which she lived in Bath.

28, 29and **30** show Sally Lunn's Refreshment House, 4 North Parade Passage, the sequence going back to the Bath of Roman times. **28** shows the house, which is the oldest in Bath, about a century ago when it was a small general store selling Rinso, Fry's cocoa, and Borwick's baking power, in particular. Today (**29**) it is one of the really notable eating places associated with the city, and now combines a museum as well.

30 is a drawing by Peter Lord showing this six-floored building in section, together with some of its fascinating details.

The date of this basically medieval building is 1482, but almost 5 ft (1.5 m) below the middle cellar floor is the floor of the original Roman house. Tiles from the hypocaust, floor tessara (mosaic), roof and flue tiles, Samian pottery and cooking equipment have all been discovered; and the tradition of hospitality goes back 17 centuries. (The Great Roman Bath is only 110 ft [33.5 m] away to the northwest.)

Who was Sally Lunn? The persecution of the Huguenots in France became merciless after the repeal of the Edict of Nantes in October 1685, and over 100,000 people made their escape over the next five years to England, Holland and Prussia. Sally was indeed a Huguenot, although reputedly leaving France about 1680, and she found employment with the baker who leased this house. She was adept at making a specially rich soft brioche, and it was so popular that it became known as a *Sally Lunn*. After her departure, the recipe was cherished, the owner keeping it in a secret cupboard. Legend has it that Ralph Allen came here from Cornwall when he arrived in Bath in 1709, and he built his town house behind it (*see* **4**). It is a fascinating building, and no one should miss the opportunity of eating one of its wares, sometimes called 'a giant muffin'.

30

31

31 and **32** Beaufort Square, sometimes called Beauford, is a small intimate place which was built between 1727 and 1736 by architect John Strahan, who came to Bristol about 1726 and set up in practice as a land surveyor and builder. He became an accomplished architect and designed Redland Court, Bristol, in 1735 – an essay in pure Palladian style – for John Cossins, a wealthy London grocer who retired to Bristol in 1732.

Strahan's client in Bath was John Hobbs, a rich Bristol timber importer who pioneered the River Avon Navigation between Bristol and Bath begun in 1712. (Kingsmead Square nearby was another example of civic planning commissioned by Hobbs and built by Strahan.)

31 shows no. 20 *c.* 1890, with a group of Victorian children, while **32** shows this house and adjacent no. 19 today, in an excellent state of preservation. The pleasant old Victorian gas-lamp has gone, but another of its type exists on the opposite side of the street.

32

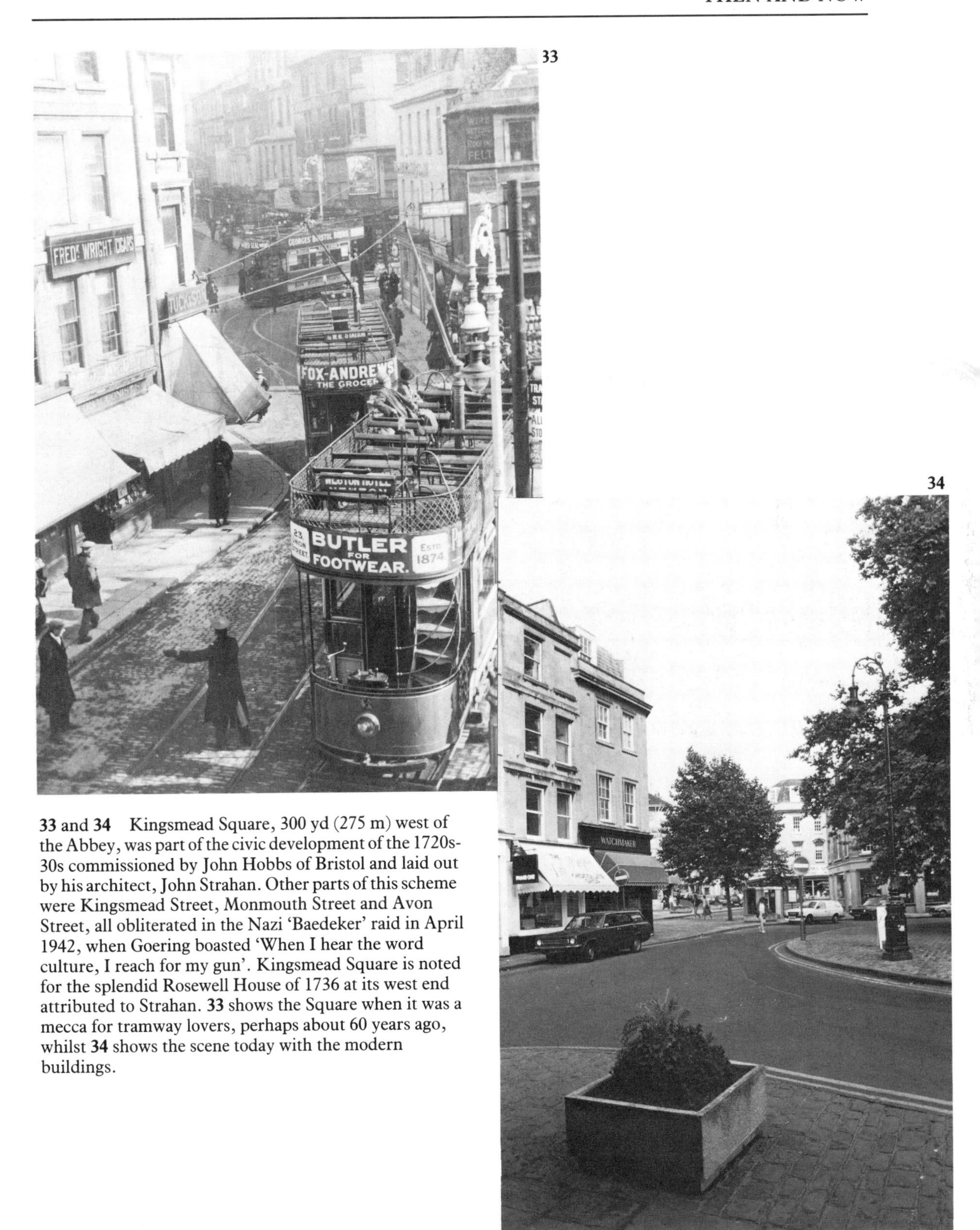

33 and **34** Kingsmead Square, 300 yd (275 m) west of the Abbey, was part of the civic development of the 1720s-30s commissioned by John Hobbs of Bristol and laid out by his architect, John Strahan. Other parts of this scheme were Kingsmead Street, Monmouth Street and Avon Street, all obliterated in the Nazi 'Baedeker' raid in April 1942, when Goering boasted 'When I hear the word culture, I reach for my gun'. Kingsmead Square is noted for the splendid Rosewell House of 1736 at its west end attributed to Strahan. **33** shows the Square when it was a mecca for tramway lovers, perhaps about 60 years ago, whilst **34** shows the scene today with the modern buildings.

35 and **36** Pulteney Bridge takes its name from Sir William (Johnstone) Pulteney, who envisaged the development of a fashionable suburb in the parish of Bathwick, on the east side of the River Avon, in which he was an aristocratic landowner. A private Act was obtained to build the bridge, and the design was entrusted to the very fashionable architect of the day, Robert Adam (1728-92). Indeed it is his only work in Bath. The completion date was *c.* 1774, and the inspiration for the project was the Ponte Vecchio in Florence. Pevsner remarks 'It is a surprisingly small bridge, with shops on both sides, and ought to be reserved for pedestrians'.

35 shows the bridge in 1901 with two hideous timber 'sheds' attached to its walls at each end. Across the central pediment is an advertisement proclaiming 'Madame Hamilton, Corset and Belt Maker'.

36 shows the bridge today. The sheds and the big chimney stack adjacent to the pediment have gone, as has the advertising board, but the silhouette of this unique bridge is marred by a modern block beyond it.

The great weir was constructed in 1972, and the Parade Gardens on the left date from *c.* 1885. This is one of the loveliest views in Bath.

35

36

37 and **38** St James Church was built in Henry Street in 1768-9, during the period when Bath was the city of Smollet and Sheridan after the death of Beau Nash in 1761. The architect was John Palmer, who completed the Pump Room in 1799. It was a spacious classical building with a western tower. In 1843, George Manners and his partner Gill, architects of Bath, added the steeple with an octagon top, with fanciful shaped pinnacles at the four corners.

37 shows this church, *c.* 1920, when Henry Street had its trams, although no overhead wires can be seen. Sadly, the church was demolished in 1957, and the street today (**33**) has a completely different look, lined with modern buildings of little character.

37

38

39

40

41

39, 40 and **41** The enterprising Midland Railway, centred on Derby, opened its London terminus at St Pancras in October 1867, and an old map of the system shows how its tentacles stretched out far and wide. From Kettering across to Cambridge in Great Eastern territory, and from Birmingham southwestwards into Bristol.

In August 1869, the railway opened its 10 mile (16 km) long branch from Mangotsfield, on the main line, into a splendid terminus in Bath, shown in **39**, a photograph of perhaps 80 years ago.

In July 1874, a new railway, jointly owned by the Midland and the London and South Western, the Somerset and Dorset, was officially opened from this station to Bournemouth over the Mendips. The line ran due west from the station for half a mile (1 km), then turned 180 degrees in a great U-bend, and then another 45 degrees to enter the noisy, dirty, Combe Down tunnel under Ralph Allen park. The gradient of 1 in 50 must have made locomotive crews suffer greatly. Up to the end of 1947, the line and station were jointly owned by the Southern and LMS railways. Then Southern Region (BR) ran it until 1963, when it passed to Western Region who promptly ran down the service so that it closed in March 1966.

The station had been a centre for railway enthusiasts because of the variety of engines to be seen there. David Lloyd says of this station, variously known as Green Park or Queen Square 'one of the most nearly perfect architecturally'; indeed its principal street elevation, shown in **40**, might have come from John Wood. Pevsner remarks 'The design is indeed creditable'; but who was the architect?

Thankfully it was not demolished after closure and was magnificently restored by Sainsbury's in 1980-82. **41** shows its present interior.

42

42, 43 and **44** On 7 March 1833, the young Isambard Kingdom Brunel (*see* Bristol **54**) was appointed engineer to the Great Western Railway. He was only 26 years old. On 31 August 1840, the eastern end of the Bristol-Bath section of the railway was opened with a fine station at Bath, having an overall roof not dissimilar to his terminus at Bristol. **42** shows this splendid building, with its broad gauge rolling stock, drawn on stone by the railway artist John Cooke Bourne (1814-96) in 1840. Ten months later, Box Tunnel was completed and the line opened to London. The station was virtually unaltered for over 50 years, until the roof was removed about 1896, after which the station looked like any other large GWR station.

43 shows the up-platform on an August day in 1897, the two seated passengers on the right-hand side of the photograph looking contentedly at the camera. The old gentleman with his curved bowler and 'beaver' is typical of the period, whilst the woman has beside her a tin hat-box.

44 is of the same platform in August 1986. Not much has changed, but the station name has become Bath Spa.

43

44

WELLS

Then and Now

The Anglo-Saxon Chronicle states: 'AD 728. This year Ina went to Rome and there gave up the ghost. He was succeeded in the kingdom of Wessex by Ethelbard who held it fourteen years'. Ina was king of Wessex between 688 and 728, and was both a Christian and a statesman. He pushed the western frontier of his kingdom into Somerset to about as far as Glastonbury, and his legal code shows a real desire to deal justly with the Celtic people who were his subjects. It is considered that in his time a church had been built at Wells, for the location was right for the foundation of a settlement at the foot of the Mendips where lead had been mined in Roman times, and where limestone and timber were to be had in abundance. As with all limestone areas, water was also plentiful, and the inhabitants would have been sustained by the water of Ina's well, afterwards St Andrew's, as they are to this day.

The *Chronicle* refers to Ina's death in AD 728, which actually took place in Rome, whence he had gone on a pilgrimage, and his memory is preserved in the inscription of his name in the floor of the cathedral near the pulpit. The settlement of Ina's Wells was in the diocese of Sherborne created in AD 704, but two centuries later, in 909, the 'Sumorsaetas' were granted their own bishop, and Wells was raised to cathedral status, the first bishop being Athelm. That he was blessed with leadership is indicated by his transfer to the Primacy at Canterbury in 923 on the death of Archbishop Plegmund. His successor at Wells, Wolfhelm, followed him to Canterbury in 926.

A singular event took place near Wells in 878 when Saxon and Dane were at war on English soil. King Alfred's victory over the Danes at Ethendun was followed by the baptism of the Danish leader, Guthrum, and a feast in the royal manor of Wedmore a few miles to the west of Wells. This has often been called the Peace of Wedmore and, to quote Dr Richard Malden, the Dean of the Cathedral, writing in 1934 – 'England was saved at Wedmore and it is ultimately to what happened there that we owe the fact that King George V is seated on the throne of England today'. Alfred's patron saint was Cuthbert, and it is possible that the church of that name in Wells was founded by King Alfred *c.* 880.

After the death of King Ethelred II in 1042, his youngest son, Edward, became king until his death on 5 January 1066. He was pro-Norman in speech, by education and in sympathy. He was, in fact, far-sighted, as events proved.

He invited many foreigners to England in order to fill high places in his kingdom, and among them was the last Saxon Bishop of Wells, Giso, born in Lorraine. Being at least half-French, if not Norman, he occupied the see of Wells from 1061-88. The Normans were sophisticated, preferring towns, and nine centuries ago Wells was little more than a village. Giso's successor, Bishop John of Tours, removed his seat to Bath and changed his title to the (first) Bishop of Bath. He had been rewarded for years of service as chaplain to William Rufus, enjoying the personal confidence of the sovereign, and thus secured the grant of Bath Abbey, transferring the see there and setting up his episcopal throne in the Abbey church. He even purchased the whole city from the king for £60 to consolidate his position therein He died in 1122 and was succeeded by Bishop Godfrey.

The cathedral establishment at Wells, like York, was never monastic and was served by a body of secular canons governed by a chapter or college. The word *chapter* comes from the Latin *capitulum*, little head, the great head being the bishop. At Bath, where their bishop was at the seat of power, there was a powerful Benedictine Abbey where King Edgar had been crowned in 973. In 1192 the monks of Bath tried to usurp the canons of Wells by electing their own bishop, Savaric, who then became Bishop of Glastonbury, taking a new title – 'Bishop of Bath and Glastonbury' – thus cutting out Wells entirely. Glastonbury Abbey was then in the process of being rebuilt after the Great Fire of 1184.

This dispute over the bishop caused great contention and argument between monks and canons about electoral rights and questions of procedure and title. Both claimed that the bishop should have his see and be enthroned in *their* church, from which alone he should take his title. The dispute was long and tempers were frayed. It was not until 1219, 14 years after Savaric's death, that Bishop Jocelin (1206-42) ceased to be Bishop of Bath and Glastonbury, by Papal decree, becoming only Bishop of Bath. It was his successor, Roger, who returned to Wells in 1242, and Pope Innocent IV decreed in 1245 that his title should be *Bath and Wells*.

Despite these ecclesiastical *contretemps*, the great cathedral at Wells as we know it today was started *c*. 1175 during the episcopate of Bishop Reginald, who died in 1191. Eight generations were to pass before the work was complete, with the building of the north tower on the west front *c*. 1425.

Sir Nikolaus Pevsner says of the cathedral in his *Buildings of England, North Somerset and Bristol* (1958):

> Of Wells it can be said without hesitation that it was the first English building in which the pointed arch was accepted throughout. Wells still stands in all its thirteenth-century glory, less interfered with than most cathedrals in England.

One of its glories is the great West Front, containing about 400 statues, 150 of them life-size or larger, described as a sculptured pageant of kings, saints and nobles – a great reredos in effect, originally containing a mass of colour.

The building was erected on a water-logged site (the Bishopric of Bath and Wells has been called the wettest in England!) and after the central tower was heightened *c*. 1320, the extra weight on the piers began to prove too much. In 1338, the chapter were summoned to deal with the situation, described as the 'shattered condition of the fabric'. The remedy was the insertion of the great strainer or scissor arches between 1338-48 to transfer the weight of the tower from west to east, where the tower piers sank on the western side. They are a remarkable feat of medieval engineering and can be described architecturally as two intersecting ogee curves, or an arch standing on its head on a normal arch.

At the time of the religious upheaval in the sixteenth century, the first definite indication of change in Wells was the receipt by the chapter of an order from Henry VIII requiring the members to accept Thomas Cromwell as their dean.

The forces that brought about the Reformation had been gathering for at least 200 years. In 1518, Thomas (Cardinal) Wolsey was enthroned as Bishop of Bath and Wells, replacing Hadrian di Castello, who lived at the Papal court in Rome. Both bishops may never even have been to Wells, and Wolsey held other sees and abbacies both in England and in France, his immense income being used to build his enormous palace at Hampton Court in Middlesex, starting in 1514. It became the largest house in England. When Wolsey was translated to the richer see of Durham, he resigned from Bath and Wells. Such abuse of the sees was halted by the Reformation.

Cromwell, Earl of Essex, had been in the service of Wolsey, and had then entered the king's service; he was elected to the privy council, made a secretary of state and, in 1536, vicar-general and vice-regent in all matters of religion. He took a delight in suppressing the monasteries, and it was fortunate, therefore, that Wells was not a monastic foundation, or its fate would have been that of so many great churches.

He obtained the deanship at Wells in order to suppress one of the wealthiest abbeys in the kingdom, the Benedictine foundation at Glastonbury, whose value was appraised at £3500 per annum.

The last abbot, Richard Whiting, was a saintly man and a beneficent power in the countryside around Glastonbury. He refused to surrender to a tyrannical decree, so Cromwell arranged for him to be falsely tried on a charge of embezzlement, and barbarously executed on Glastonbury Tor, 15 November 1539. A few months later, Cromwell was imprisoned, attainted on charges of treason, heresy and extortion, and executed on Tower Hill 28 July 1540.

Archbishop Laud, martyred on 10 January 1645, was the bishop in Wells for the two years 1626-8, and the hatred of the Puritans who put him to death is shown in this note on the title page of a book in Wells Cathedral Library – *Ludolphus de Vita Christi* – 'On Wednesday 10th May 1643, being Ascension Eve, Mr Alexander Popham's souldiers [he] being a Coronell [colonel] for the Parliament, after dinner rusht into the church [cathedral] broke down the windows, organs, font, seats in the quire, the bishop's see [throne], besides many other villainies'.

The saintly Thomas Ken (the older spelling was Kenn), a man of Berkhamsted in Hertfordshire, became bishop in 1685, but was one of the famous seven bishops who stood out against the king, James II, in 1688, and was imprisoned in the Tower with the Primate and the others. Although they were acquitted at their subsequent trial in June of that year, and James fled the country six months later, Ken felt unable to take an oath of allegiance to William of Orange, and was deprived of his see.

An interesting fragment of history is that the royal letter directing the chapter to elect the new bishop is signed *Marie R*, the co-sovereign with Dutch William. The new man was Richard Kidder, Dean of Peterborough.

On 11 or 12 November 1703, a great gale swept across Britain from the Atlantic. It was still blowing with absolute ferocity a week later, and then continued for yet another week. The following day, the people sighed with relief at the cessation of the wind; but at midnight of 26-27 November, the greatest storm ever recorded in these islands struck, and it is considered to be probably the only time that the British Isles has felt the force of a China Sea typhoon. The fury came between 2 and 5 am, the huge wind starting in the southwest, veering west then northwest, and then backing southwest. As one writer said, it was 'like a colossal cosmic ray, determined that none should escape'.

Daniel Defoe travelled the land to ascertain the destruction: £150,000 of damage in Bristol warehouses; 800 houses blown to smithereens, and thousands seriously wrecked; over 1000 country mansions badly damaged by the fall of chimney stacks; 400 windmills down; the lead roofs of 100 churches stripped off, with seven spires blown down; 150 ships sunk, and hundreds of thousands of trees blown down. Bishop Kidder and his wife were in their bedroom in the Palace at Wells when a chimney stack collapsed and fell onto the bed. Within days the price of roofing tiles in London leapt from £1 to £6 per 1000.

Kidder's death was regarded in some places as a mark of divine displeasure at his appointment, and a year later the anniversary was ordered by the soveriegn to be kept as a day of fasting and humiliation throughout the whole land.

Ralph Allen, the 'Man of Bath', was born in 1693 in a cottage on the Tregrahan estate near St Blazey in Cornwall. When he came to Bath in 1710 he lived for a time in the village of Claverton, 2½ miles (4 km) southeast. It was in this village that John Skinner was born in 1772.

In 1797 he went up to Oxford, where he was ordained. He served as curate in Claverton for a short period, but became rector of Camerton in the Somerset coalfield in 1800 until his death in 1839. He made an excursion in the autumn of 1797 through part of Somerset, Devon and Cornwall, with a companion, Le Marquis de Kermel, a French émigré, and kept a diary of it, published by the Ex Libris Press in 1985. Skinner gives us this portrait of Wells written on 21 September 1797:

> Early this morning we crossed the Mendip Hills, breakfasted with my brother William at Wells. I was afterwards examined for Priest's Orders by the Sub-Dean, Mr Moss, who desired me to preach the Ordination Sermon the following Sunday. Wells is pleasantly situated in a fertile country and I find it was a Bishop's See, as far back as the year 605, and subsequently united to Bath about the year 1138. The Cathedral was originally founded by King Ina about the year 704 but such considerable alterations were afterwards made by the then Bishop Fitz Joceline that it may be almost called his work . . . The west front is decorated with a profusion of images of Kings and Warriors . . . The Deanery and other good houses surround the area . . . and the Bishop's Palace retains its original castellated form, being encompassed by high walls and a moat. The interior is fitted up in a modern style . . . a very comfortable residence suitable to the revenue of the See, computed at nearly six thousands pounds per annum. Having perambulated this quiet city until dinner time we walked in the evening to a remarkable cavern called Wokey Hole.

Twenty years after the death of the Reverend John Skinner, the railway arrived in this quiet city. The date was 15 March 1859 and it was a short branch line from Glastonbury on the Somerset Central Railway from Highbridge. Three years later, the East Somerset arrived with its line from Witham, a station opened in 1856 on the GWR line between Frome and Yeovil. Yet a third one was to come when the Bristol and Exeter (post GWR) opened its branch from Yatton on the Bristol-Taunton main line, via Cheddar, to a station at Wells Tucker Street in April 1870.

This small cathedral city thus originally had three stations, all connected; but by the early 1960s, before the Yatton-Witham line was, sadly, abandoned in 1963, Tucker Street was the terminus for trains from Yatton, and Priory Road (the original SCR station) for trains from Witham, although only 440 yd (402 m) apart. In the 1939 timetable there was one through train a day from Witham to Yatton, the 31½ miles (51 km) taking 80 minutes, and six trains a day on the little 5 mile (8 km) long branch line from Wells Priory Road, via Polsham, into Glastonbury on the Somerset and Dorset, the journey taking eight minutes. This branch was abandoned as early as 1951. Those were the days of splendid steam locomotives, sometimes of ancient vintage, and even older carriages in rural Somerset. It has practically all gone, save Priory Road goods shed, now a listed building.

Dr Richard Malden was appointed Dean of Wells in 1933, and the following year in his book *The Story of Wells Cathedral*, describing a visit to Wells, he wrote

> If the visitor has followed the route suggested, he will have seen a collection of medieval buildings unrivalled in England and probably unsurpassed in Europe. And they are not ruins. With the exception of the vicar's hall, every one of them is in regular or constant use. It is not easy to find a place where continuity of history is exhibited more strikingly or upon a larger scale.

On 8 May 1318, a feast of St Michael, when the fabric of the cathedral was stated to be in an alarming condition, the Fraternity of Saint Andrew was instituted with a view to obtaining contributions from every parish in the diocese. This organisation lasted until about 1700, and was revived in 1933 under a new title – 'The Friends of Wells Cathedral' – each friend being asked to subscribe, *if possible*, 5/s (25p) per annum. It was set up because the annual sum then required for the cost of labour and material to maintain the fabric totalled £1200. It had recruited 320 members by 1935. The hope of its founders was fully realised for, in 1985, £292,523 was voted for the maintenance of the fabric of this glorious cathedral and its adornments.

In 1920, at the beginning of the motor age, Wells had a population of 4500. In those days the tariff of the Mitre Hotel in Sadler Street read thus: 'Breakfast 2/6; Lunch 3/-; Dinner 3/6; Bedroom 3/- per night; Chauffeur all in 7/6; Garage gratis'.

In the 1960s, the Council for British Archaeology listed the city as one of special national importance since it has an ancient town-well preserved, is a major ecclesiastical site, and has numbers of buildings of historic importance worthy of preservation and representative of the medieval and Georgian periods. Its population was then 5800.

This medieval town has long been recognised universally as one of outstanding architectural and historic importance, having the largest concentration of buildings listed under the Town and Country Planning Act, in the modern county of Somerset.

As a place of such interest, it attracts large numbers of tourists from all over the world, many being brought by organised tours. Whereas the coming of the railway did not materially affect the growth of the city, the last 60 years has seen considerable expansion to such a degree that the medieval city has become engulfed in recent housing development. One source gives its population in 1980 as 9000, and if it grew to 15,000, the local planning authority (Somerset County Council) states that it would place great strain on local land resources and raise important issues in relation to safeguarding the character of the city. The Council has stated that, in its opinion, there is every reason to restrict the population to a maximum of 11,000. Moreover, if the character and charm of Wells is not to suffer irreparable harm, an adequate solution to its traffic problems must be found and implemented.

The site of the beautiful cathedral has been holy ground for thirteen centuries. It and all its associated buildings represent devotion, labour, skill and sacrifice spread over generations. Today's generation is asked to maintain unimpaired the heritage bequeathed to it from past ages.

At the outset of a planning inquiry in southwest England in the autumn of 1985, the Inspector appointed by the Secretary of State for the Environment announced that by order of the Government, the decision he would make would be in favour of the appellant unless it could be conclusively proved that it was in the public interest for him to reach a different decision.

If one translates this in terms of a hideous tower block (as seen in Bristol) set in the middle of Wells, desired by a greedy speculator, with a government unsympathetic to the *raison d'être* of planning, what a responsiblity it throws on to the shoulders of conservation groups such as CPRE, let alone those of elected councillors and their advisers, to prove otherwise.

A visit to Wells today is a delight for anyone who enjoys such a place and has an eye for architectural detail and historic townscape. Finish in the superb cathedral and then enjoy an excellent meal in the restaurant so thoughtfully provided by the cathedral authorities in the west cloister. It is an amenity that could never have been envisaged by Dean Malden in those more staid days of 1933.

1

2

1 The eastern end of the northwest side of the medieval Market Place (fifteenth-century) was photographed about 60 years ago, and from the shadows, early in the morning. The cannon, probably a Russian 24-pounder, was captured at Sebastopol in the Crimean War, and allocated to Wells by the War Office. It arrived in 1858 and was sited on Palace Green inside the gateway leading to the Palace. After a second move, it was placed in the Market Place in 1885. A ballistics expert reports that it could not have been fired safely from the mounting shown on the photograph. The gun was finally broken up by the Ministry of Works in February 1943 at the time of the scrap-metal drive.

2 is almost the same view taken from the first floor of the Crown Hotel in July 1985. Note especially that many windows of the nineteenth century have been replaced with sashes and glazing bars, giving a far more harmonious effect. An example is the admirable first and second floor windows of the building flying the Union Jack. This picture typifies the splendid feeling that Wells imparts.

3 This splendid photograph of the Market Place was taken from a glass negative made by the Wells photographer Mr Phillips *c.* 1890. The Gothick Fountain, or Conduit, replacing an earlier one, was erected in 1797, the design by Charles Harcourt Masters. He was born in 1759, the son of a goldsmith, and was an architect and surveyor in Bath; he was paid £150 for the work in 1798.

In 1451, there was an agreement between Thomas de Bekyntone (Bishop Beckington) and the burgesses to provide water for the city, and the Bishop's Register of 1459 gives details of how the water was engineered to pass from St. Andrew's Well underground into the Market Place. In 1796, the Corporation agreed that the medieval conduit 'near the High Cross' be removed and another built on a new site. The bishop tried to obstruct the rebuilding until he received a grant of land equal to that occupied by the new structure (shades of Trollope!), but a legal opinion rejected his claim, citing the original grant of 1451.

3

4

5

6

4 The same view in August 1986, but the Market Place is full of market stalls. The cannon has long since departed, to provide more stall space. A busy market day scene, such as this must have been a feature over the centuries. The gateway at the right-hand edge of the picture is the 'Bishop's Eye', the fifteenth-century gateway that led into the Bishop's Palace, also built by Beckington, who was a great benefactor to the city.

5 shows the east end of the Market Place between the Penniless Porch (*see* **23** and **24**) and the Post Office, *c.* 1925. The serenity of this scene is in strong contrast with **6**. What is the cart doing minus its horse outside the Porch?

6 The congestion caused by mass tourism in 1985 has somehow left the character of the old buildings unimpaired. Note the office building on the right side of Penniless Porch: it has been refaced with tile hanging and reduced to two floors with three dormer windows in the roof. The Post Office is still on its old site, and the same electric light column is in both pictures.

7

7 The noble western tower of St Cuthbert's church stands 122 ft (37 m) high, and was built *c.* 1450. In medieval times the citizens of Wells were expected to attend here for their congregational worship. It replaced an earlier central tower.

It is perhaps the finest tower in Somerset, a county of splendid church towers by any standard. This photograph was taken *c.* 1930.

8 The ravages of time and weather necessitated a large restoration scheme in 1985, expected to cost £250,000.

8

9

10

11

9 When Bishop John de Villula succeeded Giso as bishop in 1088, he transferred his see to Bath. The cathedral regained its status under Bishop Robert, *c.* 1150, and the cathedral chapter was established. Other canons lived nearby, and Vicars' Close was built soon after 1347 for housing the Vicars' Choral, who have been part of this cathedral establishment since *c.* 1140. The close was completed by 1363, and the chimneys raised and crowned *c.* 1470. Note the horse-drawn delivery cart half-way up the street. This photograph dates from 1927.

10 This beautiful close, often said to be Europe's oldest complete street, is shown in 1985. At its north end is the chapel built by Nicholas Bubwith, bishop 1407-24. Note a Vicar Choral child (perhaps) walking to school.

11 The 1984 Civic Trust Award plaque records the splendid endeavours of the Somerset County Council, the Government, Church Commissioners and the Dean and Chapter to preserve this unique place.

12 and **13** These two photographs, taken about 55 years apart, serve to indicate the marvellous serenity of the Wells townscape. The field in the foreground of the older picture has become part of the large Blue Schools complex today, but the old pavilion seems to have survived. One 'brutalistic' high-rise building inserted into this scene would utterly ruin it.

12

13

14

15

14 and **15** These photographs, dating from *c*. 1928 and 1986, show the gatehouse to the Bishop's Palace. The only change in 60 years appears to be the removal of the old louvred chimney pot above the gateway and the loss of the tree to the left of the building inside the garden. The Palace was built during the episcopate of Bishop Jocelin (1206-42), but a quarrel in the next century led to the fortification of the Palace with this castle-like gate and drawbridge, and a moat. The builder was possibly Bishop Ralph of Shrewsbury (1329-63), who founded the college of Vicars' Choral.

At the time of the Great Riots in Bristol in October 1831, over general discontent about the Reform Bill, the Bishop's Palace there was destroyed by the mob, and so the Bishop of Bath and Wells wisely gave orders to pull up his drawbridge. This was the last recorded instance of it happening.

The gatehouse bell is still rung at mealtimes by a swan, its ancestor having been so taught in 1850 by the daughter of Bishop Eden, who had been Bishop of Sodor and Man, later Lord Auckland.

16 and **17** Wells is one of the few ancient English cathedrals which contains no Norman work. Bishop Jocelin built most of this magnificent West Front in the first half of the thirteenth century, giving the building the description 'possibly the finest example of Early English architecture'. The church was dedicated on 23 October 1239, three years before Jocelin's death.

The southern of the two western towers was completed *c.* 1390 by means of a legacy from Bishop Harewell, and the northern one by a similar bequest from Bishop Bubwith about 35 years later.

Over 50 years ago, about the date of **16**, the Dean, Dr Malden wrote: 'The stone of which the church is built comes from Doulting eight miles to the east, where the quarries are still worked. It is a limestone, unfortunately rather soft, so that repairs to the fabric are almost continuous'. **2** shows scaffolding against the southwestern tower in 1985 that bears witness to the Dean's words, and **17** is a close-up of mason Reginald Hughes working on the stonework by the west door in June 1985.

16

17

18

18 Dr Malden wrote in 1934: 'The sculpture (on the west front) will bear comparison with anything seen in any church. At the highest point is our Lord enthroned. The upper part of the figure has unfortunately disappeared.' The photograph shows the lower part of the figure now known as The Knees, the bottom stone of a 2-stone sculpture, since it was not possible to quarry a piece of Doulting stone 8 ft (2.5 m) tall. Its date may well be *c.* 1240-50.

The total weight of the stones was not less than three tons, and they simply stood under their own weight. How or why did the upper stone fall? The cathedral archivist, Mr. L.S. Colchester, considers that it must have been the result of an earth tremor, since there have been recorded instances of these, one being as late as 1902.

19

20

21

19 This shows the great 8 ft (2.5 m) statue of Christ carved out of Clipsham (Rutland) limestone by David Wynne and given by some of the Friends of Wells Cathedral as a special gift to mark their Golden Jubilee. It was taken from the Cathedral Green using a long telephoto lens. An Emeritus Professor of English at Oxford wrote of the work: 'I thought the sculpture looked splendid, a fine thing to be associated with a work of such distinction'. The asterisks on either side of Christ are indeed seraphim and are David Wynne's interpretation of Isaiah 6: 'the Lord sitting upon a throne, and above him stood the seraphim each had six wings'. Below them are medieval statues of the Apostles.

20 was taken at the unveiling of the statue on 28 June 1985, and shows H.R.H. The Prince of Wales with the Bishop on the left and Dean Mitchell on the right. To the left of the dais are the Precentor, the Treasurer, the Archdeacon of Wells and the Head Virger.

21 What was probably a special occasion for the people of Wells and surrounding district was the commissioning of a Church Army Mission Van outside the west door of the cathedral on a snowy day in December 1898, shown in this Phillips photograph. Note the long skirts, bowler hat and the dog at the foot of the buttress. To the right of the West Front is the upper part of the west cloister built in the thirteenth century.

22

23

24

22 Another special occasion on the Green in front of the cathedral, this time on a sunny summer day, 15 June 1985, when H.R.H. The Princess Alexandra inspected soldiers of the Light Infantry of which she is Colonel-in-Chief.

23 The name of the Victorian photographer in Wells appears in this photograph that was probably taken about 90 years ago. It is of the Penniless Gate at the northeast corner of the Market Place, one of the entrances into the Cathedral Green. It was built during Bishop Beckington's episcopate (1443-65) and derived its name from the beggars who congregated there to waylay people for alms on their way to and from the cathedral. The Bishop's rebus, a tun surmounting a beacon, is carved on the side of the gate. The name of Mr. A.J. Mawer, Solicitor, appears in a window to the right of the arch.

24 A photograph of about the same date taken from inside the gateway, with an old man sunning himself, may be compared with the same view today (**25**). Little has changed, and the same window in the Town Hall appears on both.

25

26

26 Phillips made this portrait in about 1897, on a glass negative, of a splendid 6-horse charabanc outside the Town Hall. The group has 40 persons all told, and if all were going on board for an outing, no wonder that six horses were required, for the weight must have been very great.

The Town Hall was built in 1779 by Edwin & William Lush of Salisbury, who probably also designed it, on the site of a canon's house, and it replaced the original Market House built in 1667 (demolished in 1779) that stood in the Market Place. The Town Hall originally had a flat façade with nine windows, but in 1861-4 the projecting section that gave a *porte-cochère* was built, probably designed by Henry Knight of Wells. On the first floor was the Council Chamber.

27

27 The same view in 1985, though the horses have been replaced by motor cars. This splendid Georgian public building retains the glazing bars in the windows (unlike so many buildings in Bath), but changes have occurred. A comparison of the two photographs shows that there is now a balcony on console brackets, the stone facing has been rusticated, three of the first floor windows have drip mouldings, and the central window has been altered to form an access to the balcony, from which, no doubt, the Mayor could distribute largess to the assembled crowd below!

It now transpires that the well-known London architects, Caroe and Passmore, were entrusted with the reconstruction of the portico, since it had not been properly bonded into the main building in the 1860s. This was in 1932-3, and they used the old stonework, adding a few embellishments.

28

28 is another Phillips photograph of about 1895, taken in Wells Cattle Market in Princes Road. Note the apple-seller and the curved Derby bowler hats worn by most of the men, the younger boys sporting cloth caps. In the nineteenth century, Wells cheese market was the largest in the west of England, and the advertisement board of J.C. Way and Sons, Cheese Factors, stands to the right of the mill chimney.

29

29 A 1985 view. In these days of a shrinking railway system and centralisation of many functions, the cattle market has departed to Shepton Mallet, and its site has become a car park.

30

30 A GWR publication of 1934 contains an advertisement for the Swan Hotel in Sadler Street (in 1451 written Sadelerstrete) that asserts 'established in the reign of King Edward III' (1327-77). Here is an excellent Phillips plate of the main façade in Sadler Street, dressed overall with hundreds of fairy-light candles for the Diamond Jubilee of Queen Victoria in the high summer of 1897. To the right of the hotel are the premises at no. 13 of Messrs. Wicks and Son, Upholsterers and Undertakers.

31

31 Here is the hotel photographed 88 years later from further back on Cathedral Green. It is almost unaltered.

32

32 This Phillips plate was taken in Palace Fields and shows a Volunteer Group marching through them with several bands. Note the delighted small boys running alongside. The date on the plate is 14 March 1898, but surely the trees would not have been almost in full leaf in early spring? In front of the cathedral can be seen part of the ruined section of the Bishop's Palace, when the Sovereign (Edward VI) removed the lead roof to replenish his coffers!

Except for a few missing trees, the view remains the same today, and people still walk through the park on their way from Wells to Dulcote.

33 shows the last train to run on the former Somerset and Dorset Railway branch line to Wells, about to leave Glastonbury Station on 29 October 1951. The engine is no. 41296, one of 130 class 2 MT 2-6-2(T) locomotives built at Crewe about 1951, to a design by the last chief of mechanical engineer to the LMSR, H.G. Ivatt. Her sister, no. 41298, has been preserved by the Quainton Railway Society in Buckinghamshire at Quainton Road Station.

34 depicts that sad day, 9 September 1963, when the last freight was about to depart from Wells Tucker Street for Yatton. The fireman is about 'to water the beast', pulling over the long leather chute from the water column. To his right the tank flap is open. The engine is no. 82037, one of 45 class MT 2-6-2(T) locomotives designed and built at Swindon from 1952 onwards. Not a single one of this class has survived. One wonders if the historic nature of the occasion was impressed upon the small boy.

33

34

35

35 and **36** Almost a century elapsed between the Frith photograph in **35** and the contrasting one in **36**. Here is depicted the serenity of one of Britain's most magnificent cathedrals, reflected in the water that comes from the springs near the Bishop's Palace that gave the city its name.

Bibliography

Bath, Portrait of a City – Paul Hardy and William Lowndes

Buildings of England, North Somerset and Bristol – Sir Nikolaus Pevsner (1958)

West Country Tour – John Skinner (1985)

The New Bath Guide – Eva Jolly (1985)

Bath – R.A.L. Smith (1944)

The Story of Wells Cathedral – Dr Richard Malden (1934)

Victorian Buildings in Bristol – Clare Crick (1975)

Walking in Bristol – Helena Eason (1984)

Portrait of Bristol – Keith Brace (1971)

Somerset – Maxwell Fraser (1934)

Somerset – Ralph Whitlock (1975)

Railway Stations and Halts in Avon – Mike Oakley

Historic Towns in Somerset – Aston and Leech

The Past All Around Us – Readers' Digest (1979)

Brunel's Bristol – R.A. Buchanan and M. Williams (1982)

Great Western Kings – C.J. Freezer (1984)

Bristol Official Guide – (1929)

Bath Walks within the Walls – Peter Smithson (1971)

Britain under the Romans – S.E. Winbolt (1945)

English Social History – G.M. Trevelyan (1942)

The Caliph of Fonthill – H.A.N. Brockman (1956)

Railways of the Western Region – Geoffrey Body (1983)

Changing Bristol – Tony Aldous (1979)

The Stratford and Midland Junction Railway – J.M. Dunn

Index

Abona, Roman settlement 9
Adam, Robert 82
Aelphege, Abbot of Bath 83
Agricola, Julius 52
Akemancester 53
Aldhelm, St, of Sherborne 53
Alexandra, HRH The Princess 104, 105
Allen, Ralph 54, 57, 61, 78, 90
Anglo-Saxon Chronicle 9, 53, 88
Aquae Arnemetiae (Buxton) 52, 69
Aquae Sulis (Bath) 52, 53, 59, 69
Arnolfini Arts Centre 17
Athelm, Bishop of Wells 88
Auckland, The Lord Bishop 99
Austen, Jane 60, 76
Avonmouth Dock 14
Avon River Navigation 57, 79

Baldwin, Thomas 56, 62, 71
Bath
    Abbey 53, 54, 64, 65, 66, 67, 88, 89
    Assembly Rooms 56, 57
    Beauford Square 56, 79, 80
    Colonnade 62, 63
    Gray Street 76
    Georgian development 56
    Hot Springs 52, 58, 59, 69
    Kingsmead Square 81
    Milsom Street 71
    Museum of Costume 57
    Oliver Biscuit 55
    Orange Grove 67
    Paragon, The 60
    Preservation Trust 74
    Pulteney Bridge 82
    Pump Room 56, 59, 62, 83
    Queen Square 11, 58, 75
    Railway Station GWR 86, 87
    Railway Station MR/S&DR 84, 85
    Roman Baths 68, 69, 70
    Royal Crescent 56, 74, 75
    Theatre 56
    Trim Street 56, 72, 73
Bath & Portland Stone Firms 69, 70
Beckford, W.T. 58
Beckington, Thomas, Bishop 94, 95, 105
Benson, Martin, Bishop of Gloucester 25
Betjeman, Sir John 9
Bindon, John 15
Bird, William, Prior of Bath 64
Blackburne, William 39
Blisworth Canal Tunnel 14
Bodley, George 16, 45
Brace, Keith 9, 12, 15, 19, 23, 38, 48
Brendon, St 34
Brennas and Belinus 31
Bridges, James 40
Bright, Robert 13
Brislington Roman villa 9
Bristol
    Abbey 10, 35, 43
    All Saints Church 38
    Art Gallery 15
    Assize courts 15
    Bridge 40, 41
    Cabot Cafe 43, 44
    Cathedral 10, 13, 35, 43, 44
    Central Library 16
    Christ Church 37
    City Docks 48
    College Green 10, 43
    Corn Exchange 11
    Dialect 17
    Diocese 10, 13, 43
    Floating Harbour 49
    Georgian development 11
    Grammar School 27
    growth of city 17
    Guilds 10
    High Cross 10, 11
    Hospital of St Bartholomew 26, 27
    Hospital of St Peter 16
    Park Street 32, 33
    Riots 12, 17, 99
    St James' Place 20
    Slave Trade 11, 12, 18
    Theatre 11
    Tramways Centre 46, 47
    University 15, 32, 33, 36
Bristol Society of Architects 14
Browne, George, Bishop of Bristol 13
Brunel, I.K. 12, 13, 14, 49, 50, 58, 86
Brydon, J.M. 64
Bubb, J.G. 19
Bubwith, Bishop 97, 100
Busby, C.A. 19

Cabot, John and Sebastian 10
Cabot Tower 34, 35
Calais Muster 10
Camerton 52, 91
Caroe & Passmore 108
Caroline of Brunswick, Queen 75
Castello, Hadrian di, Bishop 89
Catherine of Braganza, Queen 23, 54
Cattybrook Bricks 15
Celtic mining 52
Charter House lead mine 69
Christmas Steps 27
Civic Trust 97
Clarkson, Thomas 12
Claverton 90
Clifton, All Saints Church 45
Clifton College 15, 45

Clifton Suspension Bridge 12, 13, 14
Clipsham limestone 103
Coalpit Heath 13
Colchester, L.S. 101
Collett, Charles 51
Colston Centre 17
Colston Hall 15
Commercial Rooms 19
Constantine 53
Cook, Ernest 57
Coombe Down 54, 57, 85
Copperhouse Foundry 12
Corlett, Dr Ewan 14
Cotham Martyrs Memorial 10
Cromwell, Thomas, Earl of Essex, Dean of Wells 89, 90

Davis, Graham 56
Defoe, Daniel 13, 90
Doubleday, Charles 49
Doulting limestone 100, 101
Dummer village 25
Dunstan, St 53
Dyer, Charles 42

East Somerset Railway 91
Eden, F.C. 45
Edgar, King, coronation of 53, 89
Edward The Confessor, King 88
Edward VII, King 42
Ellis, Stanley 16, 17, 29

Falkland Islands 14
Fiennes, Celia 13, 54
Fitzharding, Robert 10
Fonthill Abbey 58
Foster, John 15
Francis Hotel, Bath 75
Friends of Wells Cathedral 91, 92, 103
Friese-Greene, William 76
Frith, Francis 44, 60, 63, 64, 82, 105, 115

Gainsborough, Thomas 60, 61
Garrick, David 61
Gay, Robert 76
Gerontius 53
Giso, Bishop of Wells 88
Glastonbury Abbey 54, 89, 90
Glastonbury Railway Station 91, 114
Godfrey, Bishop of Bath 89
Golden Hind 17, 49
Goodridge, Henry 58
Gough, W.V. 34
Grand Pump Room Hotel 63
Great Britain 13, 14, 48, 49
Great Western 13
Great Western Railway 13, 58, 91
Green Park Station, Bath 84, 85
Guppy, Thomas 13
Guthrum 88

Hamilton, Lady Emma 74
Hampton Court Palace 89
Hansom, C.P. 15
Harewell, John, Bishop of Bath & Wells 100
Harris, E. Vincent 35
Henwood, Luke 38
Herschel, Sir William 71
Hoare family 10, 11
Hobbs, John 79, 81
Holden, Dr Charles 16
Holloway, William 54
Hotwells 20, 23, 24, 74
Hughes, Reginald 100

Ina, King of Wessex 88
Innocent IV, Pope 89
Ison, Walter 74

Jocelin, Bishop of Bath 89, 91, 99, 100
John de Villula (of Tours), Bishop of Bath 54, 88, 97
Jolly, Edith 55, 58

Ken, Thomas, Bishop 90
Kent, Marina, HRH The Duchess of 57
Kermel, Marquis 91
Kidder, Richard, Bishop 90
Killeedy Abbey, Co. Limerick 34
King Class locomotive 51
King, Oliver, Bishop 64
Knight, Henry 107
Knights Templar 29

La Tribe & Weston 44
Laud, William 90
Lawford's Gate, Bristol 10
Lewins Mead Meeting 39
Leycester, Edward 67
Lightholer, Thomas 71
Linley, Elizabeth 56, 74
Linley, Thomas 56, 74
Liszt, Franz 57
Llandoger Trow 16, 18
Llandogo on the Wye 18
London Missionary Society 25
Lord, Peter 78
Ludgvan, Cornwall 54
Lunn, Sally 77, 78
Lush, E & W 107

McAdam, John 19
Mackintosh, C.R. 16
Malden, Dr Richard, Dean of Wells 88, 91, 92, 100, 101
Manners, George 67, 83
Margaret, HRH The Princess 74
Mary Tudor, Queen 10
Masters, George H. 94
Matthew, Robert 69
Mawer, A.J. 105
Maze, Peter 13
Merchant Adventurers, Society of 10, 12, 48
Midland Railway 85
Millerd 10
Milsom, Daniel 71
Mitchell, Peter, Dean of Wells 102, 103
Mitre Hotel, Wells 92
Morris, William 15, 57
Multon, John 67

Nash, Richard 'Beau' 54, 55, 56, 62, 67
National Trust 9, 10, 11, 57
Nazi air raids, Bath 57, 81
Nazi air raids, Bristol 16, 29, 45
Norris, Archdeacon of Bristol 13

Oatley, Sir George 15, 33
Octagon Chapel, Bath 71
Oliver, Dr William 54, 55
Order of the Sisters of Charity 16
Oswald, Bishop of Worcester 9, 53
Oxford, Jesus College 54

Palace Fields, Wells 113
Palmer, John 56, 62, 83
Paty, Thomas & William 11, 37, 40
Paul, William 38
Pearson, J.L. 13, 35
Penn, William 25

Pevsner, Sir Nikolaus 11, 15, 16, 18, 33, 34, 45, 47, 54, 56, 61, 75, 85, 89
Phillips (Wells) 94, 103, 105, 107, 109, 111, 113
Phipps, Charles 56
Pitman, Sir Isaac 74
Pitt the Elder, Earl of Chatham 61, 73
Pole, Sir Felix 51
Ponte Vechio (Florence) 82
Ponton, Archibald 15
Poole, Henry 42
Pope, Richard 47
Pope, T.S. 15
Potter, Robert 45
Pulteney, Sir William 82
Puritans 90

Ralph of Shrewsbury, Bishop of Wells 99
Rauzzini, Venanzia 76
Richardson, Sir Albert 57
Richardson, Charles 15
Robert, Bishop of Bath 97
Roman cities in Britain and Europe 53
Roman invasion of Britain 52
Royal Mineral Water Hospital 55
Royal Photographic Society 71
Royal West of England Academy 14, 15
Russell, Charles 13

St Benoit-sur-Loire Abbey 9
St Blazey, Cornwall 54, 61, 90
St Cuthberts Church, Wells 88, 96
St James Church, Bath 83
St John Baptist Church, Bristol 30, 31
St Mary Redcliffe, Bristol 10, 16, 35
St Nicholas Church, Bristol 40, 41
St Raphael's College, Bristol 16
St Stephen's Church, Bristol 47
Saunders, C.A. 13
Savaric, Bishop of Bath & Glastonbury 89
Scott, Sir Gilbert 64
Sedding, Edmund, John and Edmund 15, 16
Severin, Tim 34
Severn Tunnel 15
Shaw, Norman 15
Sheridan, Richard 55, 56, 74, 83
Skinner, John 90, 91
Smith, R.A.L. 56, 57
Smithson, Peter 57
Smollett, Tobias 55, 56, 83
Snowdon, The Earl of 74
Somerset Central Railway 91
Somerset & Dorset Railway 85
Stony Littleton, Avon 52
Storm, The Great (1703) 90
Stourhead, Wiltshire 10
Strahan, John 79, 81
Stratford & Midland Junction Railway 14
Strauss, Johann 57
Street, Sir George 13, 15, 35, 45
Sul 52, 54
Sullivan, Sir Arthur 57
Swan Hotel, Wells 111, 112

Tacitus, Caius 52
Temple Church, Bristol 28, 29
Temple Meads Station, Bristol 9, 27, 50, 51
Townesend, George 38
Trevelyan, G.M. 55
Trim, George 73
Tyley, Jabez 42

Vertue, William & Robert 64
Vespasian 52
Victoria, Queen Empress 43, 44
Victoria Rooms, Clifton 42

Wales, HRH The Prince of 102, 103
Walpole, Horace 12
Way, J.C. & Sons 109
Webb, Philip 15
Wedgwood, Josiah 76
Wedmore, the Peace of 88
Wells
  Archdeacon of 103
  Bishop's Palace 99, 115
  Cathedral 88, 89, 100, 101, 102, 103, 115, 116
  Cathedral Library 90
  Cattle Market 109, 110
  Conduit 94
  Crown Hotel 93
  Market Place 93, 94, 95
  Penniless Gate 95, 105
  Railway Stations 91, 114
  St Cuthbert's Church 88, 96
  Town Hall 107, 108
  Vicars' Close 97
Wesley, Charles 25
Wesley, John 11, 29
Westbury-on-Trym 9
Wetherell, Sir Charles 12
Whitefield, George 25
Whiting, Richard 90
Wilberforce, William 12
Willcox, William John 63
Williams, Henry 37
Wills family, Bristol 14, 15
Wills, Frank 15
Winbolt, S.E. 53
Winstone, F.R. 20
Wolfe, General Edward 73
Wolfe, General James 73
Wolfhelm 88
Wolsey, Cardinal 89
Wood, John (father & son) 11, 54, 55, 56, 61, 74, 75, 76
Wood, John 15
Wyatt, James 58
Wyatt, Sir Matthew 50
Wycliffe, John 9
Wynne, David 102, 103
Wyrecestre, William 23

York, Sarah HRH The Duchess of 25